Praise for *Trigger Warning*:

'It's strong-minded, unafraid, determined to knock down all the various specious arguments against free speech, unapologetic about insisting on the value of free expression, and terrifically well argued. In these weak-minded times it's good to have so uncompromising a defence'   SALMAN RUSHDIE

'A passionate and timely polemic'   FRANCIS WHEEN,
Mail on Sunday

Trigger Warning

Is the Fear of Being Offensive Killing Free Speech?

Concise and abridged edition

Mick Hume

WILLIAM
COLLINS

William Collins
An imprint of HarperCollins*Publishers*
1 London Bridge Street
London SE1 9GF
WilliamCollinsBooks.com

First published in Great Britain by William Collins in 2015

This William Collins abridged paperback edition first published 2016

1

Copyright © Mick Hume 2015

Mick Hume asserts the moral right to
be identified as the author of this work

A catalogue record for this book is
available from the British Library

ISBN 978-0-00-812640-7

Printed and bound in Great Britain by
Clays Ltd, St Ives plc

For Stella and Isabel, may they always think
what they like and say what they think

Trigger Warning (noun): a statement at the start of any piece of writing, video, etc, alerting the reader or viewer to the fact that it contains material they might find upsetting or offensive.

Contents

Introduction
to the concise edition

Free speech is under threat in the West. But then, what else is new? Freedom of expression has never been assured, even in its heartlands, ever since the ancient Athenians took a democratic vote to put to death their greatest philosopher, Socrates, for talking out of turn.

But the threats to free speech are always changing. The UK parliament has not yet voted to make anybody drink poisoned hemlock, like Socrates, for saying the wrong thing.

This short book is intended to highlight the new challenges to our most precious liberty in the twenty-first century. It aims to provide some ammunition for fighting the new free-speech wars.

In our Anglo-American culture today free speech is not threatened by jackbooted state censorship. The more insidious threat comes from a creeping crusade for conformism in thought and speech. The slogan emblazoned on the crusaders' banner is 'You Can't Say That!'.

It has become the fashion not only to declare yourself offended by what somebody else says, but also to use the 'offence card' to demand that they be prevented from – and possibly punished for – saying it.

The most dramatic attack on 'offensive' freedom of speech in modern times was the *Charlie Hebdo* massacre in 2015. Islamist gunmen murdered eight cartoonists and journalists and four others at the Paris offices of the satirical magazine, supposedly to 'avenge the prophet' after *Charlie* published cartoons mocking Muhammad.

The massive 'Je Suis Charlie' demonstrations that followed the massacre and the connected murders at a Jewish supermarket were uplifting displays of human solidarity that made an impression on us all. They also, however, gave a misleading impression of the state of play with free speech in Europe and America.

Here, it might have appeared, was a clear cultural divide: on one side, a free world united in support of freedom of expression; on the other, a handful of extremists opposed to liberty. Behind those solidarity banners, however, Western opinion was far less solidly for free speech.

Many public figures could hardly wait to stop paying lip service to liberty and start adding the inevitable qualifications, obfuscations and, above all, 'buts' to their supposed support for free speech. To quote the American writer Andrew Klavan, it looked like 'The Attack of the But-Heads'.[1]

It quickly became clear that the threat to freedom came not just from a few barbarians at the gate. Free speech faces more powerful enemies within the supposed citadel of civilisation itself. Those 'Je Suis Charlie' placards had hardly been cleared from the streets before another international consensus emerged, stretching from the Pope to the Chinese Communist Party and encompassing much of Western liberalism between. All agreed that the *Charlie Hebdo* massacre showed the need to restrict 'hate speech', ban inflammatory words and images and curtail the right to offend.

Thus after the mass killings committed by Islamist gunmen came the mass free-speech fraud committed by Western elites – making ritualistic gestures of support for free speech 'in principle' while hammering it in practice.

That free-speech fraud did not come out of the blue. If there really was such solid support for free speech, it would not have taken the cold-blooded murder of cartoonists to prompt our politicians and public figures to mention it. The sudden loud expressions of support for free speech were so striking because they contrasted with the everyday reality that we in the West now spend far more time discussing how to restrict free speech than how to defend and extend it.

The hard fact is that the Islamic gunmen who attacked *Charlie Hebdo* acted not just as the soldiers of an old Eastern religion. They also acted as the armed extremist wing of a thoroughly modern Western culture of enforced conformism, fighting for a highly fashionable belief in your right to suppress whatever you find offensive. The Islamist gunmen simply took that attitude to a murderous extreme.

It was the culmination of a steady loss of faith in freedom of speech and the ability of people to handle uncomfortable words or images. Since the *Charlie Hebdo* massacre it has become obvious that those who would kill free speech are winning the battle. The motto of our age is not 'Je Suis Charlie' but 'Vous Ne Pouvez Pas Dire Ca!', which roughly translates as 'You Can't Say That!'.

Free speech in Anglo-American society is under siege from three main enemies in the modern age.

- First, there are the official censors in government and the courts who want to control offensive and inflammatory speech. In the UK and Europe they are using hate-speech laws to convict thousands every year of speech crimes. Even in the US, where freedom of speech is legally protected by the First Amendment to the constitution, the principle has fallen so far out of favour among the political elite that the *New York Times* feels free to ask whether it is 'time to reconsider that constitutional line'.[2]
- Second, there are the increasingly influential unofficial censors, the witch-hunting Twitter mobs and online

petitioners pursuing and trying to silence everybody whose views are not to their taste. Often foremost among them have been the student officials and activists seeking to 'No Platform' anybody, feminist or funnyman, who might make a student feel 'uncomfortable'.

- The third enemy of free speech today is self-censorship. Under pressure from the first two, and unsure of which opinions are now acceptable or even which words they are permitted to use, many people now fight shy of expressing any strong views that might fall outside the mainstream. Those whose words stray from the straight and increasingly narrow are often quick to withdraw and apologise for any potential offence caused at the first sign of a wagging finger.

This new alliance against free speech is not only active in the traditional political sphere. It is invading areas which might once have been thought of as off-limits for censorship.

- The internet ought to be the best thing to happen to freedom of expression since the invention of the printing press. Now free speech online is under attack from Twitter mobs and social media lobbies demanding that something be done to stop them being offended by words. Whatever the pretext, the net effect is always to reduce the scope for unfettered free speech online, and waste the extraordinary opportunities offered by the internet for advancing freedom and open discussion.

For example, nobody seems certain how to define a troll, yet everybody apparently agrees that something must be done about them. This fashion for troll-hunting provides an all-purpose, all-seasons licence to police what is said on the internet. In the UK and Europe the law has joined in the international troll-hunt, and people have been charged and imprisoned for online thought crimes. Even in the US, troll-hunting has become a national blood sport, with

Twitter – previously advertised as 'the free speech wing of the free speech party' – setting up an Orwellian-sounding Trust and Safety Council to police the tweets.

To claim that you have been 'trolled' has become a sign of virtue through victimhood. To be outraged by trolls offers those attacked confirmation that they are in the right – and an excuse to attack the right to free speech online. Nobody has to read, listen to or take seriously what some twit tweeting from his mum's back bedroom has to say. We should be free to ignore them or respond in kind. But nobody should have the right to use the label 'troll!' as a gag to silence those opinions they don't like online.

- Universities should be citadels of open-minded inquiry and freedom of speech. Yet, remarkably, the university campus has become a major new front in the war on free speech, on both sides of the Atlantic. What's remarkable is not that academic freedoms are under assault – they have been threatened by outside forces since the first European universities were established in the Middle Ages. What beggars belief is that it is now students and academics themselves who are joining campus authorities in trying to impose new limits on free speech and free thinking in UK and US universities. Far from being ivory-towered bastions of freedom, our universities have come to see themselves more as a womb-like fortress to protect young people from dangerous words and ideas.

The world has been turned upside down so that those who think of themselves as liberal- or even radical-minded are in the forefront of the attack on free speech in colleges. In the name of making universities 'safe spaces', student activists have demanded bans on 'offensive' speakers and comedians, books and videos, statues and sombreros. 'Safe Space' policies sound like unopposable mom-and-apple-pie policies. Who wants to make anywhere an 'unsafe space'? The question is, however: safe from what? These policies go far beyond threats of violence or intimidation, to cover any opinion or language that some students may not like.

Apparently students must now 'feel comfortable' at all times. But if that was really all young people wanted, they surely could have stayed at home, tucked up safe and warm with their mums and dads. Restricting college life to students' pre-set, safe comfort zone risks closing the door on the new – and worse, closing young minds.

Those supposed liberals attempting to ban views they find offensive might do well to recognise the historical company they are keeping. Two hundred years ago, fellows and students at Oxford University also took direct action to No Platform offensive opinions. They burned a pamphlet that, says one account, had caused 'maximum offence', while the university authorities expelled the author from Oxford. He was the nineteen-year-old Percy Bysshe Shelley, and the Romantic poet's 'little tract' that caused such lofty outrage in 1811 was called *The Necessity of Atheism*. It would surely be better for today's protesting students to try to follow in the footsteps of the taboo-busting Shelley rather than the Oxford conservatives and censors who banished the offensive student and his opinions from university life.

- Entertainment might once have been considered a world where people could crack jokes or sing songs that were outside the rules of 'respectable' society and everyday life. No longer. The new free speech wars are being waged in some unlikely places, such as British football and the comedy scene on both sides of the Atlantic.

The campaign to rid football of offensive, improper and abusive language marks an extraordinary turnaround. Football was long ungoverned by the etiquette of everyday life, accepted as the home ground of what Sigmund Freud called 'the id', the more emotional, irrational side of the human psyche, where it was accepted that people could let rip and take a break from the rules of polite society.

By contrast the campaign to sanitise football has now reached the point where fans can be afforded even less free speech than they would be elsewhere in life. The Scottish government's Offensive Behaviour at Football and Threatening Communications (Scotland) Act has created an extraordinary situation where a Rangers fans has been jailed for four months for the crime of singing an offensive song in a Glasgow street.

Comedy too has come under the watchful eye of the you-can't-say-that culture. Good jokes are often in bad taste, mocking the respectable rules and morals of society, pushing at the limits of what passes for taste and decency in any era. There have long been attempts to control what is deemed 'acceptable' humour and to censor what is not.

However, as with other issues in the Anglo-American free-speech wars, the terrain has shifted. Once the complaints were about blasphemous and indecent comedy. Now the protests are more often against comedians accused of breaking the new taboos – racism, sexism, homophobia, transphobia, Islamophobia, anti-Semitism and the other usual suspects.

Comedy is a messy business, and people can laugh at the most outrageous things. The wish to dictate not just what jokes a comedian should tell, but also what we should laugh at, is the clearest conceivable attempt at thought control. What could be more intrusive than trying to police something as reflexive as a snort of laughter? The trends towards more conformist comedy put at risk one of the most important forms of release we have left in a dour world. This is no laughing matter. If comedians are not allowed to upset and offend, what chance have the rest of us got?

One other phenomenon which captures the mind-narrowing trends of our times is the onward march of the Trigger Warning, from which this book takes its title.

A Trigger Warning is an advisory label stuck at the front of a book, article, film or whatever to warn students that this work involves words or images that may traumatise them in some way.

They have spread from US colleges across the Atlantic and the internet. Defenders of Trigger Warnings will argue that they amount to little more than a few words to help preserve the vulnerable from harm. But the truth is that those few words speak volumes about the parlous state of freedom.

Trigger Warnings were initially conceived as an online therapeutic tool to help victims in discussion forums for sufferers from Post-Traumatic Stress Disorder (PTSD). If somebody posted about a particularly violent or distressing experience, others could be forewarned that reading such a post might 'trigger' a traumatic memory and reaction in them.

Even conceived in these narrow terms, experts tell us, the concept of Trigger Warnings appears unconvincing. Extend the Trigger Warnings away from PTSD sufferers to books read by university students or films watched online, however, and the whole thing becomes a dangerous nonsense. Post-Traumatic Stress Disorder was developed as a category to describe the psychological effects suffered by those exposed to the horrors of war, violence or other extreme experiences. What has that to do with students or others being made to feel uncomfortable by some 'naughty' references in literature?

But while the causes might be slight, the consequences could be more serious in terms of the future of free speech and open discussion. Once the notion of trauma is reduced to 'feeling uncomfortable', the sky is surely the limit for Trigger Warnings. Today we are advised that students should be allowed to opt out of some classes and warned about reading classics from *The Great Gatsby* to Ovid's *Metamorphoses*. Tomorrow the demand might be to stop teaching such 'triggering' texts altogether – and that list could stretch from Shakespeare to *Game of Thrones*, with much in between. As wags have observed, why not put TWs on Trigger Warnings, to warn that they are about to mention sex or violence?

Trigger Warnings are a model of how all the talk about harm and vulnerability and comfort can become a coded way of undermining both sides of free expression – the freedom to speak or write what you like, and the equally important freedom to read or listen and judge for yourself. That should be the most serious warning of all to anybody who feels 'uncomfortable' at the undermining of freedom of speech.

In response to all this we need to take an uncompromising stand for unfettered free speech with no buts, bans, prison sentences or guns to the head. That must mean defending it as an indivisible liberty, for all or none at all. Free speech is always primarily about defending what a US Supreme Court justice once described as 'freedom for the thought that we hate'.

Those who campaign on free-speech issues often see them as rights to be defended for high-minded dissidents in faraway places. The notion of demanding free speech closer to home for, say, tabloid hacks, vulgar internet 'trolls' or uncouth sports fans would horrify many a British civil liberties lobbyist (emphasis on 'civil', as in well-mannered, rather than liberties, as in free-for-all).

Yet there are important reasons in principle and practice why we need to defend free speech for all. A universal liberty cannot be divided. Once we allow free speech to be questioned for some then what should be right instead becomes a privilege, to be doled out from above like charity to those deemed deserving. And when it comes to 'selective' censorship, one thing always leads to another.

'Hate speech' just means moral views you object to, and one person's hate speech is another's passionate belief. As some university campaigners have discovered to their consternation, if you seek to No Platform those you find offensive, don't be surprised if somebody does the same thing to you. Those who live by the ban can perish by it, too.

It might be tempting to imagine going along with attempts to crack down on 'radicalisation' and censor Islamist or Islamophobic extremists. But in practice, such simple authoritarian solutions won't work. Trying to defend freedom by banning its enemies, to uphold our belief in free speech by censoring those who disagree, is worse than useless and can only add credence to their cause.

What we need to do is to fight them on the intellectual and political beaches, not try to bury the issues in the sand. Free speech is the potential solution, not the problem.

I first wrote in defence of 'the Right to be Offensive' more than twenty-five years ago, when I was the editor of long-deceased *Living Marxism* magazine. Our slogan then – 'Ban Nothing – Question Everything' – has informed my attitude ever since. In the intervening years, free speech has fallen further from favour. The first edition of *Trigger Warning* was published shortly after the *Charlie Hebdo* massacre, to highlight the pressing need to defend free speech. That has become a more urgent problem since. We have also, however, witnessed the prospects of turning the tide and winning more vocal support for free speech, especially on campus.

So this is a call-to-arms to fight for free speech before it's too late. It might seem hard to make a stand when unfettered free speech is so out of fashion. It often means having to stand up for the rights of some unattractive types whose views we don't want to hear. But that is what makes it so important today.

The fact that many feel there are now few principles worth fighting for in political life makes it all the more imperative that we should stand for free speech for all. Because free speech is the indispensible midwife of new ideas. If our society is ever to find a way out of its current malaise, we need an open, no-holds-barred debate about everything. We need, in short, more free speech rather than less. Including, like Socrates, the right to say the 'wrong' thing.

A few things we forgot about free speech

No subject (with the possible exception of football) has been talked about as much yet seriously discussed as little as free speech. Everybody pays lip service to the right to freedom of speech. Few of us appear to give much thought to what that means or why it matters. Sometimes it's necessary to remind ourselves of the obvious and look again at what we take for granted.

After all, it's funny how the simple little things can slip your mind. The first thing that seems to have been forgotten about free speech is that it's supposed to be Free. The second thing that is often forgotten is that it's simply Speech.

The third thing we often forget is that, when you put those two words together, you have the most important expression in the English language. Free speech is the single most powerful factor in creating and sustaining a civilised society. Without the advance of free speech, the development of life as we know it in the West is unlikely to have been possible over the past 500 years.

In short, without the willingness of some to insist on their right to question everything and to speak what they believed to be true, we might still be living on a flat Earth at the centre of the known Universe, where women were denied the vote but granted the right to be burnt as witches.

To begin with the dreaded f-word. It often appears to have slipped our Anglo-American society's mind that free speech is supposed to be Free. That's free as in 'free as a bird', to soar as high as it can and swoop as low as it chooses. Not as in 'free-range chicken', at liberty only to scratch in the dirt within a fenced-in pen and en route to the chopping block.

Free means speech should not be shackled by official censorship imposed by governments, police, courts or any other state-licensed pecknose or prodstaff. Nor should it be stymied by unofficial censorship exercised through university speech codes and 'safe spaces', twitterstorming mobs of online crusaders against offensiveness, or Islamist zealots gunning for blasphemy. And nor should it be sacrificed by the spineless self-censorship of intellectual invertebrates.

If it is to mean anything, free speech has to live up to its name. This is the hardest thing for many who claim to endorse the principle to remember in practice. It means that what others say or write need not conform to what you, I, or anybody else might prefer.

Here is the terrible truth about free speech. Anybody can choose to write, blog, tweet, chant, preach, phone a radio programme or shout at a television set. Not all of them will have the purity of soul of Jesus Christ or Joan Rivers, the wisdom of Socrates or Simon Cowell, or the good manners of Prince Harry or Piers Morgan. That's tough. They still get the same access to free speech as the rest of us, whether we like it or not.

Defending the unfettered Free in free speech is not a question of endorsing whatever objectionable or idiotic things might be written or said. Nobody had to find *Charlie Hebdo*'s cartoons insightful or hilarious in order to stand by its right to publish them. Nor is it a question of being soft and suffering somebody else's nonsense in silence. Free speech means you are also free to talk back as you see fit.

The Free in free speech does mean recognising that free speech is for fools, fanatics and the other fellow too. Like all true liberties, free speech is an indivisible and universal right. We defend it for all or not at all.

Remembering to put the Free in free speech makes clear why we should oppose attempts to outlaw or curtail certain categories of speech. Freedom is, unfortunately, indivisible. You cannot have half-freedom, part-time freedom or fat-free freedom. You cannot abolish slavery but only for white people or celebrities. Similarly you cannot declare your support for free speech, but only defend those parts of it that you like or that meet your preferred set of standards, however high-minded those preferences might appear.

In all the talk about free speech today, how often do you hear free speech spoken of as a universal and non-negotiable right? Instead the focus seems always to be on the buts, the exceptions, the limits to freedom. Everybody in public life might insist that they support free speech, but scratch the surface and it becomes clear that what many support is not so much free speech as speech on parole.

They want speech that is released from custody only on licence with a promise of good behaviour, preferably wearing a security ankle bracelet to stop it straying from the straight and narrow. Speech that is free to toe the line, stick to the script and do what it is told. The reinterpretation of freedom to mean liberty-on-licence is a con that the free-speech fraudsters should not be allowed to get away with.

Once you forget the meaning of 'freedom' and start cherry-picking which people or what type of speech might deserve it, free speech ceases to be a right. Instead it becomes a privilege, to be extended or withheld to the well- or the not so well-behaved as those in authority see fit. This is the message of all those fashionable sermons about how 'rights come with responsibilities'. That is just another way of saying that it is not a right at all, but a selective reward for good behaviour. Rights don't come with buts or provisos.

Once you make free speech a privilege and not a right, who are you going to trust to make the decision about where to draw that line through free speech? Government ministers? High court judges? Mary Berry and Sharon Osbourne?

This problem is even more acute now, when everything is judged by the subjective standards of 'offence' and things can be censored or banned not for threatening public order but for hurting somebody's feelings and making them feel 'uncomfortable'.

It is important to remember that free speech in the West was never an act of largesse doled out by governments. From the Magna Carta 800 years ago to today, any liberties that are worth the parchment they are written on have been hard-won in a struggle to wrest them from our rulers. Once won, those liberties do not come with any moral commandments. Nobody has to pass through the eye of an ethical needle to qualify for the right to free speech. There should be no official test to pass or licence to obtain before you can express an opinion. Liberties do not come with strings attached, any more than freedom can be exercised in leg-irons.

It is to be dearly wished that people exercise their rights responsibly and take responsibility for what they say. We might like to think that taking responsibility would always involve saying what you mean and meaning what you say; expressing the truth as you understand it as clearly as you are able, and then standing by it for all that you are worth. But wishing that could be true is no excuse for trampling on the speech rights of others in the name of what you imagine their responsibilities should be.

We should remember that the Free in free speech is not only about the freedom to speak and write as you see fit. It is also about the freedom of the rest of us to hear and read everything that we choose, and to judge for ourselves what is right. The flipside of freedom of speech is the freedom to listen (or not) and to choose.

By restricting the free-speech rights of those you detest, you weaken your own and everybody else's freedom to listen and to argue, to test the truth and judge for ourselves.

As Thomas Paine, the English radical who became a key figure in both the American and the French revolutions of the eighteenth century, wrote in the introduction to his classic *The Age of Reason* (a critique of religion considered so offensive that it was subject to serial prosecutions by the British government): 'He who denies to another this right, makes a slave of himself to his present opinion, because he precludes himself the right of changing it.'[1] It is not only those directly denied their freedom who are 'enslaved' by selectively chaining some forms of speech.

We are under no obligation to take any notice of anybody's words; the right to free speech never entails a 'right' to be taken seriously. But nor does the speaker have any obligation to restrict what they say to what we want to hear. To mean something worthwhile, freedom must be first and foremost for the other person's point of view. George Orwell put in perfectly in his 1945 essay 'The Freedom of the Press' (originally written as a preface to his novel *Animal Farm*, though ironically the publisher refused to include it): 'If liberty means anything at all, it means the right to tell people what they do not want to hear.'[2]

As part of forgetting to put the Free in free speech, we also appear to have forgotten the meaning of tolerance. Today tolerance is talked about in two related ways: either it means allowing the expression of views without judging or criticising them, or it is used as the excuse for closing down views which are too offensive, as in 'we will not tolerate intolerance'. Neither has much to do with true tolerance.

Intolerance is always the enemy of free-thinking. But tolerance and the right to free speech does not mean a free ride. Tolerance is not about allowing anybody to rant away, offend and insult without challenge because 'everybody's entitled to their opinion'. True tolerance means allowing others to express their opinions, however disagreeable – and then being free yourself to tell them what you think of it, just as they are free to repay the compliment to you. In this, I am always with the great Englishman of letters Dr Samuel

Johnson, who declared that 'Every man has the right to utter what he thinks truth – and every other man has the right to knock him down for it.'[3] Figuratively speaking, at the very least.

The second thing we have forgotten about free speech is that it is Speech. It is simply words. Words can be powerful tools, but there are no magic words – not even Abracadabra – that in themselves can change reality. Words are not deeds. It follows that offensive speech should not be policed as if it were a criminal offence.

It is true that 'words can be weapons' in a battle of ideas, or even just in a slanging match. But however sharp or pointed they might be, words cannot be knives. However blunt words are, they are not baseball bats. No matter how loaded they are or how fast you fire them off, words are not guns.

Yet all too often today we see words treated as if they were physical weapons. People in the UK are imprisoned for tweeting insults, as if they had handed out a bodily beating. Outraged online mobs pursue 'rape deniers' or other speech deviants across social media much as the London mob pursued the misogynist murderer Bill Sykes through the Dickensian city. Politicians and public figures in the US or UK are forced to apologise for having caused unintentional offence with some words, as if they had unintentionally caused a war (which is something they would never apologise for, of course).

Words can hurt but they are not physical weapons. And an argument or opinion, however aggressive or offensive it might seem, is not a physical assault. There are and should be laws against assault and threats of violence. There often are but should not be laws or rules against words used to express opinions, however violently one might disagree with them. The right response to violent assault is to end it, as forcibly as necessary, and possibly to lock up the perpetrator. The answer to bad words is not to end speech or lock up the speaker. It is more speech – to resist or simply to rubbish the words objected to.

But should all speech really be free? Is it really possible to draw such a firm distinction between offensive words and criminal offences? The answer is yes, once we are clear what we mean by free speech as encompassing all forms of expression from ideas and opinions, through invective and insults, to jokes or mindless jabber.

There are other types of speech that the most liberal-minded among us have long considered to be indefensible: direct threats of violence or blackmail, for example, or malicious defamation of individuals, or illegal obscenity such as child pornography. Even the US First Amendment has not protected these forms of words.

But these are not really arguments against free speech. In properly distinguishing between words and deeds, we need to make a distinction between words that are simply speech – the expression of an idea – and words that instead become part of an action – the execution of a deed. For instance there is a big difference between expressing a general violent hatred of the government or minority groups, and deliberately inciting, provoking or organising specific acts of violence against particular institutions, individuals or groups. The first category is speech, to be tolerated, like it or not (but challenged as you see fit). The second is something other than free expression, and we do not have to put up with it.

Those who support free speech have long sought to distinguish words from deeds and to have legal exceptions to the principle overturned or at least defined as narrowly as possible.

The trouble is, however, that in wider discussion in the Anglo-American world today, things are moving in the opposite direction. The tendency now in politics, the media and academia seems always to try to broaden, rather than narrow, the grounds on which words should arguably be kicked out from under the free-speech umbrella.

The insistence that 'This is not a free-speech issue' has become a staple expression of the free-speech fraudsters, as a way of maintaining their alleged support for the principle whilst shafting it in practice. Once, the phrase 'This is not a free-speech issue' might justifiably be heard only in response to something as serious as a direct threat to kill – or just something as trivial as a request to make less noise in a bar or on the bus. Now we hear it used promiscuously in response to all manner of questions that obviously *should* be 'free-speech issues', from demands for new laws against nasty internet 'trolls' to bans imposed on controversial political speakers or comedians on campus. It can seem as if some would like to turn the exception to free speech into the rule.

But what about incitement? Inciting somebody to commit an offence is a crime. Offering an offensive opinion or inflammatory argument should not be. In a sense all arguments are 'inciting' – as in urging or provoking – somebody to do something, whether that means to change their opinion or the brand of coffee they drink. Those on the receiving end are still normally free to decide whether to do it. We should be very wary of criminalising speech so long as all that is being chucked about are words.

And what about offensive and hateful speech? These issues are addressed later. To begin with let us simply remember that in Western societies it is usually only those consensus-busting opinions branded offensive or unpalatable that need defending on the grounds of free speech. Nobody ever tries to ban speech for being too mundane. This is not a question of celebrating extremism or obnoxiousness. It is simply a matter of recognising that, when it comes to upholding the principle of free speech in practice, if we look after those opinions branded extreme, then the mainstream will look after itself.

Free speech is more important than hurt feelings. As recently as 1999 David Baugh, a leading black American civil liberties lawyer, defended a Ku Klux Klan leader who had been charged after a cross-burning, gun-toting rally. The attorney assured the jury that he was well aware that his client and the KKK hated black men like him. But that, Baugh argued, did not alter the racist's free-speech rights: 'In America, we have the right to hate. And we have the right to discuss it.'[4]

Baugh lost that cross-burning case on a point of law. Today he might be widely considered to have lost his mind. Yet he was right. In a civilised society, if we are talking about thoughts and words – however vitriolic – rather than violent deeds, all must be free to hate what or who they like, whether that means Muslims, Christians, bankers or Bono. To seek to ban the right to hate should be seen as no less an outrageous interference in the freedom to think for ourselves than a tyrant banning the right to love. The best way to counter hatreds and ideas we despise is not to try to bury them alive, but to drag them out into the light of day and debate them to the bitter end.

There is a good reason why it's important to remember the meaning of both Free and Speech, however uncomfortable they might make us. Because the third thing we tend to forget about free speech is that it is the most important expression in the English language.

To borrow a phrase from the techies, free speech might be called the 'killer app' of civilisation, the core value on which the success of the whole system depends.

Free speech is the voice of the morally autonomous individual, nobody's slave or puppet, who is free to make his or her own choices. It is the spirit of the age of modernity on full volume, first captured more than 350 years ago by the likes of Spinoza, the great Dutchman of the Enlightenment, who challenged the political and religious intolerance that dominated the old Europe and set the standard for a new world by declaring that 'In a free state, every man may think what he likes and say what he thinks.'[5]

Free speech is not just about individual self-expression. It is the collective tool which humanity uses to develop its knowledge and understanding, to debate and decide on the truth of any scientific or cultural issue. Free speech is also the means by which we can bring democracy to life and fight over the future of society, through political engagement and the battle of ideas.

Free speech is not just a nice-sounding but impracticable idea, like 'free love'. It has been an instrumental tool in the advance of humanity from the caves to something approaching civilisation. It is through the exercise of free speech and open debate that individuals and societies have been able to gain an understanding of where they want to go and why. The open expression of ideas and criticism has often proved the catalyst to the blossoming of creativity.

That's why history often suggests that the freer speech a society has allowed, the more likely it is to have a climate where culture and science could flourish. Even before the modern age of Enlightenment, those past civilisations that we identify with an early flowering of the arts, science and philosophy, from Ancient Greece to the Golden Age of Islamic civilisation in the Middle East and Spain, had a disposition towards freedom of thought and speech that set them apart.

The advance of free speech has been key to the creation of the freer nations of the modern world. Every movement struggling for more democracy and social change recognised the importance of public freedom of speech and of the press for articulating their aims and advancing their cause.

One sure sign of the historic importance of free speech to liberation struggles is the instinctive way that tyrants have understood the need to control it to preserve their power. Thus during the struggle over slavery in America in the nineteenth century, the slave-owning classes did all they could to suppress any public discussion of slavery as a means of keeping control. Southern states outlawed criticism of slavery and used gag rules to prevent the US Congress in Washington even discussing anti-slavery petitions. As the anti-slavery campaigner (and former slave) Frederick Douglass said in 'A Plea for Free Speech in Boston', after an 1860 meeting to discuss the abolition of slavery was attacked by supposed gentlemen in that civilised northern city, 'Liberty is meaningless where the right to utter one's thoughts and opinions has ceased to exist. That, of all rights, is the dread of tyrants. It is the right which they first of all strike down. They know its power ... Slavery cannot tolerate free speech. Five years of its exercise would banish the auction block and break every chain in the South.'[6]

History-making movements and individuals have demonstrated that if not for the fight for free speech, other freedoms would not be possible. Without the ability to argue your cause there would be no way to clarify your aspirations, make clear your demands, or debate how best to strive for them.

More recent struggles for freedom and equality in Western societies were just as intimately bound up with freedom of speech. The demand for free speech, for the right for their voices to be heard, has proved central to the struggles for women's emancipation, gay liberation and racial equality in the UK and US. There is a grim irony in the fashion for feminist, trans or anti-racist activists today to demand restrictions on free speech as a means of protecting the rights of the identity groups they claim to represent. Without the efforts of those who fought for more free speech in the past, these illiberal activists would not be free to stand up and call for less of it in the present.

Free speech at its best has involved the freedom to challenge the most ardent orthodox beliefs of the day, regardless of whose toes that might tread on. That is why the essence of free speech is always the right to be offensive. Those who would deny the right of others to break taboos, offend against the consensus and go against the grain of accepted opinion would do well to remember where we might be without it.

Anybody suggesting now that the Sun circles the Earth would be accused of insulting our intelligence. Yet even four centuries ago, the notion of God's Earth orbiting the Sun as a mere satellite and acolyte was among the most offensive ideas possible to Europe's ruling religious and political powers, and they condemned as heretics the likes of Bruno and Galileo who suggested it. It would be hard to imagine anything more offensive in twenty-first-century Western society than trying to deny votes to women or demanding the reintroduction of legalised slavery. Yet not so very long ago those who opposed such oppression were being arrested and worse for offending against the state or nature in our Anglo-American civilisation.

The right to be offensive is not about the freedom to fart in a restaurant, or to yell drunken abuse in the street, or to direct personal insults at the Pope's or anybody else's mother. Heat and passion are important. Being honest and above all clear in what you say, however, is usually more important than just being loud or lairy. Being passionate about your argument need not necessarily involve being profanely rude to the other side (although it might).

But the right to be offensive is really about what you say rather than the way you say it. It is about having the liberty to question everything; to accept no conventional wisdom at face value; to challenge, criticise, rubbish or ridicule anybody else's opinion or beliefs (in the certain knowledge that they have the right to return the compliment to you).

This is what makes the right to be offensive so invaluable, the cutting edge, the beating heart, of freedom of speech and of the press. What, after all, would be the point of those freedoms if you were only at liberty to say what somebody else might like? How could it be a right if it was withdrawn the moment you choose to use it to say what others consider wrong?

Remembering why free speech matters so much should lead us to demand more of it rather than less.

In recent years it has been easy for civil liberties lobbyists in the UK and Europe to appear rather smug about free speech on the home front. They could go about banging the drum on behalf of free-speech martyrs in China or Iran, whilst pointing out that, in our societies, freedom of expression had been made safe by the European Convention on Human Rights (ECHR), incorporated into UK law under Tony Blair's New Labour government by the 1998 Human Rights Act, which enshrines the right to freedom of expression.

In fact the ECHR and the Human Rights Act embody the attitude of 'free speech, but …'. As the leading UK textbook on civil liberties and human rights says, the legal conventions 'recognise that the exercise of these freedoms comes with special responsibilities, and so may be subject to restriction for specified purposes'.[7] As soon as you attach legal responsibilities, never mind special ones, a freedom ceases to be a right.

That problem is spelt out by a glance down the list of the 'specified purposes' for which the ECHR, supposed stone tablet of European liberalism, concedes that freedom of expression can legitimately be restricted:

> The exercise of these freedoms, since it carries with it duties and responsibilities, may be subject to such formalities, conditions, restrictions or penalties as are prescribed by law and are necessary in a democratic society, in the interests of national security, territorial integrity or public safety, for the prevention of disorder or crime, for the protection of health or morals, for the protection of the reputation or rights of others, for preventing the disclosure of information received in confidence, or for maintaining the authority and impartiality of the judiciary.[8]

It is enough to make you wonder what might escape such a broad net of 'conditions, restrictions or penalties'. The 'public safety' and the 'protection of health and morals', for example, sound like the sort of catch-all excuses for restricting free speech beloved of dictators down the decades. It is the restriction of speech in the name of freedom. And it is ultimately up to the learned judges of the UK and European courts, of course, to decide just how much liberty to allow.

In the US, the First Amendment to the Constitution sets out a far clearer commitment to free speech, stating baldly that 'Congress shall make no law … abridging the freedom of speech, or of the press'. Those fourteen words set a global gold standard for free-speech law that has still to be equalled anywhere in the world more than 200 years later.

Some of us in the UK get called 'First Amendment fundamentalists' for arguing that we could do with a First Amendment-style hands-off attitude to free speech over here. It is not meant to be a compliment, but to imply that there is something of the dangerous extremist about embracing the spirit of the First Amendment. That is a sign of the times.

Yet from the point of view of this free-speech fundamentalist it is arguable that even the First Amendment does not take us far enough. Even in its own legalistic terms, it leaves the interpretation of freedom for the whole of American society in the hands of the nine Supreme Court justices. As that same authoritative legal textbook observes with lawyerly understatement, this 'still leaves the right to free speech somewhat exposed'.[9] There have been times in not-so-distant history, such as around the First World War and during the Cold War, when the Supreme Court generally took a dim view of the free-speech rights of any radical political views.

Once you step outside the legal confines of the courtroom, the power of the First Amendment to protect free speech in America is severely limited. The constitutional ban on legal censorship by the state has not prevented the proliferation of informal censorship and bans across US college campuses, for example.

Those who imagine the US safe from all this behind the all-important First Amendment forget that, even in America, the cultural tide appears to be turning against free speech. We might all do well to recall the words of the US judge Learned Hand who, speaking in 1944 at a wartime rally for liberty in New York's Central Park, warned against investing 'false hopes' in the paper constitution and the courts to protect freedom: 'Liberty lies in the hearts of men and women; when it dies there, no constitution, no law, no court can save it.'[10]

Free speech may not have died in the hearts of the men and women of the West, but it is ailing badly. Free speech is left looking like that 'free-range' chicken, fenced in and approaching its use-by date. If we want to live in a truly tolerant world we should reject every demand to cage, censor, parole or punish speech. No matter how sympathetic a case the censors make, and however much you might abhor the words others use.

Behind the universal lip service paid to the principle, if we forget the true meaning of free speech the losers will not only be those relatively few who find themselves banned or prosecuted for 'speech crimes'. We will all be the poorer for allowing the creation of a culture in which people become scared to say what they mean, development of knowledge is stifled, political debates effectively suspended, and where from the university campus to the internet we are living with a bland, 'safe' environment in which anodyne becomes the new normal.

To turn things around means dealing with new opponents of free speech today and confronting the creeping problem of the silent war on free speech – a war fought by those who claim to support free speech, but … The battlegrounds are many in this war. It is primarily a fight, not just against censorship, but conformism; not just to end restrictive laws, but to free the mind of society.

As the Victorian genius J. S. Mill says, in his landmark essay *On Liberty*, 'Protection, therefore, against the tyranny of the magistrate is not enough; there needs protection also against the tyranny of the prevailing opinion and feeling; against the tendency of society to impose, by other means than civil penalties, its own ideas and practices as rules of conduct on those who dissent from them'.[11] The consequence of what we have forgotten about free speech has been to give a free hand to those who wish to impose conformist ideas as 'rules of conduct on those who dissent from them'.

No doubt a world in which we enjoy free speech will contain ugly, difficult and hurtful ideas as well as good and inspiring ones.

But the alternative to free speech is inevitably worse. That is why free speech is always a price worth paying, and much too important to pay mere lip service to.

2

The age of the reverse-Voltaires

I believe in free speech. You believe in free speech. Everybody with more than two free brain cells to rub together in the free world believes in freedom of speech. Or so they say.

'Blasphemers' can be sentenced to death in Islamist states. The internet might be censored to near-death in Communist China. In our civilised Western universe, however, we still enjoy freedom of expression. Or think we do.

Strange, then, that so many now choose to exercise their freedom of speech in order to tell the rest of us what we can't say. When they say they support free speech 'in principle' they apparently mean on another planet, rather than in the real world.

Back here on Earth, meanwhile, the fashion is to support something called 'free speech-but', as in: 'I believe in free speech-but there are limits/-but not for hate speech/-but you cannot offend or insult or upset other people.' And the buts are getting bigger and wider all the time. As one US commentator had it in the wake of the *Charlie Hebdo* massacre, 'The "but" in the phrase "I believe in free speech but" is bigger than Kim Kardashian's [and] has more wiggle-room than Jennifer Lopez's.'[1] Those remarks would probably get him banned from speaking on several campuses for offensive 'fat-shaming'.

To imagine that you could believe in free speech 'but' not for certain opinions is rather like saying 'I believe in scientific proof, but that's no reason to rule out Father Christmas and fairies at the bottom of the garden'; or 'I believe in the equality of the sexes, but equal pay for women is going too far'. The b-word does not 'clarify' your stated belief, but effectively buts it out of existence.

Behind the headline support for the principle of free speech, the UK seems not so sure in practice; one major survey found that a larger section of the British public (64 per cent) supported the right of people 'not to be exposed to offensive views' than supported the right for people to 'say what they think' (54 per cent).[2] Perhaps more surprisingly, polls suggest that many Americans, too, might not be as certain about free speech as they once were. Washington's prestigious Newseum Institute conducts an annual survey on attitudes to the First Amendment, which alongside other liberties enshrines freedom of speech and of the press in the US Constitution. Asked whether they think the First Amendment goes 'too far' in upholding those freedoms, in 2014 38 per cent of Americans answered 'yes' – an increase from 34 per cent in 2013, and a big jump from the mere 13 per cent who said yes in 2012.[3]

A steady drip of outrage is eroding the rock of free speech. The response is even worse. On any day when cartoonists are not being murdered in Europe, few voices are raised to speak up for freedom. We seem to spend far more time discussing the problem with free speech and how to curb it than how to defend, never mind extend it. And every little extra curb on one sort of speech encourages mission-creep towards censoring another.

The freedom to think what you like and say what you think has become another empty ritual to which we just pay lip service. Even the lip service stops when somebody dares to think it is real and says something beyond the pale or the bland. People might oppose outright censorship, but a self-censoring muted conformism is the order of the day.

What's going on? There is nothing new about free speech being threatened. The modern right to freedom of speech has been under threat since the moment it was first won. It would always be true to say that 'free speech is in danger'. But there is something different happening today.

The danger to free speech in the West now comes not only from such traditional enemies as the little Hitlers and aspiring ayatollahs who disdain to conceal their contempt for liberty. More important today is the challenge from those who claim to support that freedom, yet seek to restrict it in practice. This is the new threat: the silent war on free speech.

It is a silent war, but not because its proponents are quiet – they are anything but. This is a silent war because nobody who expects to be taken seriously will admit that they are fundamentally against the right to free speech. To oppose freedom of expression has historically meant being in favour of fascism, totalitarianism and the burning of heretical books – if not of actual heretics. Few want to be seen goose-stepping out in such company today.

Instead we have a silent war on free speech; a war that will not speak its name, fought by wannabe censors who claim that they are nothing of the sort. The result is not violent repression and brute censorship, but the demonising of dissident opinions in a crusade for conformism.

The silent war is not ostensibly aimed against free speech at all. It is presented, not as a blow against liberty, but as a defence of rights: the right to protection from offensive and hateful words and images; freedom from media harassment and internet 'trolling'; the right of students to feel 'comfortable' on campus.

You will rarely hear anybody admit that they hate free speech. Instead the crusaders come up with a coded way to get that message across, and their codes can change as fast as if controlled by an Enigma machine (rather than by a student union committee meeting). You might be accused of hate speech, or told to go and 'check your privilege' (e.g. make sure you are not a white person talking about racism); or you could be accused of 'mansplaining' an issue to women, or of committing 'micro-aggressions' in your speech.

All very confusing no doubt, and easy for even a sympathetic speaker to get caught out and left behind the fast-changing tide.

But whatever coded form of words they deploy, the crusaders are really saying one of two things: either 'You-Can't-Say-THAT!', if you're attacked for what is said; or 'YOU-Can't-Say-That!' if the attack is on who said it. Or possibly, both.

But no, no, we must understand, those demanding restrictions on what others can say today are not against free speech. They are simply in favour of freedom from words that may upset or do harm. Who could disagree with such humane sentiments or fail to empathise with those facing what they deem offensive, harmful speech?

You don't have to be a Bambi-shooting bigot to defend unfettered free speech. Quite the opposite. Free speech is the lifeblood of any modern, liberal-minded society. It follows that any attempt to restrict free speech, however worthy the case might sound, imperils a liberty that has helped to make all our other rights possible.

Never mind the lip service paid to it 'in principle' by the free-speech fraudsters today. Underlying attitudes to that freedom have not simply altered in recent times. They have been turned on their head.

We are living in the age of the reverse-Voltaires. The revolutionary writer François-Marie Arouet, known by his pen name Voltaire, was a pioneer of free speech in eighteenth-century Enlightenment France. Voltaire is credited with one of the great historical sayings on the subject: 'I disapprove of what you say, but I will defend to the death your right to say it.' (In fact those words that resound down the years were not written by Voltaire, but by his biographer, Evelyn Beatrice Hall. More than a century after his death, she pithily captured the spirit of his writings for an English-speaking audience.)[4]

Voltaire's principle is a clear statement of the attitude to tolerance and free speech that characterised the Enlightenment. It recognises that free speech is something more than a personal possession, something bigger than a personal opinion. Free speech is too important to be restricted, however it might be used and abused. It is a test of any free society that, with Voltaire, we allow open debate and freedom for the thought that we disagree with or even detest.

Now, however, we have the rise of the reverse-Voltaires. The *cri de coeur* of today's hardcore offence-takers turns his principle inside out: 'I know I'll detest and be offended by what you say, and I will defend to the end of free speech my right to stop you saying it.' The reverse-Voltaires do not wish to dispute ideas or arguments that offend them. They would deny the other person's right to say it in the first place.

For the reverse-Voltaires, nothing can be more important than their personal emotions, nothing is bigger than their ego or identity. The only test of whether something should be allowed is how it makes them feel (and most important, how it makes them feel about themselves). Reverse-Voltaires cannot tolerate having their opinions challenged, prejudices questioned, self-image disrespected or toes stepped on. The result is a demand to limit free speech in the name of their right to be protected from words.

The reverse-Voltaires are as intolerant of dissent as any old-time religionists. But where the priests of yore based their intolerance on the supposedly objective authority of a supreme God above, today's would-be censors base theirs on the subjective wishes of their personal idol within. They are often self-regarding narcissists; except that where Narcissus fell in love with his placidly beautiful image reflected in a pool of water, they are in love with their angry image of permanently outraged self-righteousness, reflected in the murky pool of social media.

The champion of free speech Voltaire said (in his own words this time): 'Think for yourself and let others enjoy the privilege of doing so too.' The mantra of the reverse-Voltaires is more like: 'Think *of* yourself and don't let others enjoy the privilege of thinking any differently.'

* * *

The rise of the reverse-Voltaires, who insist on their right to stop the speech of others, marks a counter-revolution in Western attitudes to free speech.

Until a few hundred years ago intolerance was the accepted orthodoxy of the ruling elites in a straitjacketed European society. The belief in free speech first emerged in modern Europe and then America not as an abstract ideal, but as the expression of a newly envisioned freedom in society.

Freedom of speech was conceived as a way for individuals, groups and entire nations to defend their interests against overbearing political or religious authority. It was not only about people having the right to express themselves. It was also about exposing the use and abuse of power, and holding the powerful to account.

That was why the demand for free speech and a free press was at the heart of the movements for democratic government first in England, then in America, then continental Europe. It was why free speech was spoken of in terms of a battlefield defence.– as a 'bulwark' or a 'fortress' in the fight against tyranny. Free speech became the weapon that men (and later, women) would wield to defy and even to help defeat the authoritarian power of states.

That was then. This is now – a time when, rather than embracing the demand for free speech as a defence against the power of the state, many demand that the authorities use their powers to suppress the 'offensive' or 'harmful' speech of other people. Voltaire the free-speaking revolutionary has been replaced by reverse-Voltaire, the radical crusader against excess of freedom. Where once the danger was seen as the state's control of speech, now free speech running wild is the threat proclaimed.

How have we come to this? Attitudes to free speech almost always reflect our attitudes to people, and how much freedom we believe they should have. The growing mistrust of free speech partly reflects the declining faith we hold in humanity.

In Anglo-American society today a therapeutic concern with protecting emotions is often seen as more important than a clash of ideas. People are perceived and often perceive themselves as vulnerable, capable of being either harmed or incited to harm others by words alone. The view of humanity as vulnerable, thin-skinned and ultra-sensitive makes free speech appear more dangerous today. In the twenty-first century you can draw moral authority from your status not only as an old-fashioned warrior or a leader, but more often from claiming public recognition as a victim. That elevation of vulnerability into a virtue has clear implications for attitudes towards the liberty of others to indulge in offensive speech.

As people become more wary of one another, free speech has become something to fear, an unpredictable spark that could start a conflagration. The worries about too many words roaming around freely without constraint is really a fear of people being allowed to say and hear what they choose without the guiding hand of a parental figure or policeman.

The reverse-Voltaires are demanding the right to be cocooned against the discomfort caused by other people's words running riot. And they are quite prepared to use official or unofficial forms of censorship to get their way.

We might think that we live in an age when, at least in Western societies, there is less repressive government censorship than at any time in recent memory. Yet as one critic, Philip Johnston, notes, the reality is that in the non-censoring UK, 'more people are being jailed or arrested in Britain today for what they think, believe and say than at any time since the eighteenth century'.[5]

How can there simultaneously be both less censorship and more punishment of words? Because, the UK authorities will insist, the legal crackdown on what people say, especially online, is not state censorship of free speech at all. It is simply a positive attempt to protect people from harmful and offensive words.

In the USA, we are assured, there can be no state censorship of speech, thanks to the protection given by the First Amendment.

But that does not stop the politicians trying, in the cause of protecting citizens from harmful words.

No politician or official in the West, it seems, is publicly in favour of censorship today. A ban, however, by any other name still smells the same. The way that state curbs on speech can now be presented as positive, even liberating, measures is a sign of changing times. But it should not alter our attitude to censorship.

Yet the official censors of our Western governments and courts are rarely the driving force behind censorship today. The authorities more often take their lead from the army of unofficial censors demanding action against allegedly dangerous speech.

These lobby groups, individual politicians, media figures and student activists are the leading reverse-Voltaires of public life. They are often full-time offence-takers, whose default emotion (and emotions count more than ideas now) is outrage. Theirs is a free-floating sense of outrage which, while apparently reflecting a deeply held moral conviction about an issue, can quickly detach itself and move on to the next free-speech scandal.

Among the preferred tools of these crusading reverse-Voltaires are the online petition and the twitterstorm, which can create an instant impression of mass outrage with relatively little effort or substance. These unofficial measures are often sufficient to silence the targeted forms of speech. If not, their demands for official censorship will generally find a willing ear among the UK authorities.

The perma-outraged, professionally offended reverse-Voltaires are relatively few in number. Yet they punch well above their weight in terms of influencing public policy and debate – as symbolised by the disproportionate importance attached to their favourite playground, Twitter. They have helped to create an atmosphere in which standing up for a fundamental right – free speech – can be seen as extremism. It is not that most people are enthusiastic about official censorship, but many have internalised the idea that it is better not to offend than to express a controversial opinion. These are the self-censoring 'sorry majority', symbolised by politicians and public figures who will apologise and withdraw their remarks at the first sign of a wagging finger.

The reverse-Voltaires are seeking to overturn some long-established principles of free speech. Nadine Strossen, a professor at the New York Law School and former president of the American Civil Liberties Union, points out that there are two 'bedrock' principles of free-speech law in America. The first of these is 'content neutrality' or 'viewpoint neutrality': 'It holds that government may never limit speech just because any listener – or even, indeed, the majority of the community – disagrees with or is offended by its content or the viewpoint it conveys.' The second bedrock principle of US law holds that 'a restriction on speech can be justified only when necessary to prevent actual or imminent harm to an interest of "compelling" importance, such as violence or injury to others.'[6]

Twenty years ago, in a book entitled *Defending Pornography: Free Speech, Sex and the Fight for Women's Rights*, Strossen demonstrated how the radical feminist campaign for legal bans on pornography in America 'violates both of these principles', by demanding that a form of expression be restricted because of its offensive content; in order for that campaign to succeed, she wrote, 'the very foundation of our free speech structure would have to be torn up'.

The 'Nineties' would-be feminist censors might largely have failed. Two decades later, however, the reverse-Voltaires have had considerable success in tearing up the principle of 'content neutrality' and getting speech restricted on the ground that they find what it says offensive. They have not managed to rewrite the legal principles of the US First Amendment (not yet, anyway). But they have secured countless bans in practice on US and UK campuses, and shaped the British state's censoriously interventionist attitude towards offensive speech.

* * *

The silent war on free speech often appears a remarkably one-sided affair. Where are those voices prepared to speak up for freedom against all the official and unofficial censorship, and wake the sorry majority from their self-censoring slumber? There are relatively few prominent figures today prepared to stand on the shoulders of the heroes of the historic fight for free speech. The Tom Paines, John Wilkeses and J. S. Mills of the twenty-first century are most often noticeable by their absence. The outburst of rhetorical support for free speech immediately after the *Charlie Hebdo* massacre was striking precisely because it was so out of kilter with what we (don't) hear the rest of the time.

What has happened to the West's liberal lobby in defence of free speech? They are still willing to speak up for the rights of repressed dissidents in far-flung places, yet when it comes to battles on the home front, many self-styled liberals have accepted the case for restricting the 'wrong' types of speech. It is not just that they are failing to resist the assault. Many have gone over to the other side in the free-speech wars.

This war is not led by the traditional enemies of free speech. It would be easier to defend freedom of expression against old-fashioned bigots and censors. But this silent war is more often prosecuted by liberal politicians, intellectuals, academics, writers, judges and suchlike. And those who might once have been in the front rank of the censorship lobby, from religious conservatives to cranky right-wing politicians, can now find themselves on the receiving end.

This turnaround has even helped to create a situation among progressive-minded students where censorship can appear cool. Once radical youth demanded 'Ban the Bomb'. Today's generation of student activists are often more likely to be demanding that the authorities ban the book, the bloke or the boobs.

A refined-looking liberal lobby of cultural high-flyers might seem to make an unlikely mob of book-burners. But consider if you will the strange case of Monty Python's Flying Circus, Her

Majesty's Most Honourable Privy Council, and the attempt to sanitise Britain's unruly press.

In the wake of a phone-hacking scandal, over tabloid reporters listening to the voicemail messages of celebrities, public figures and high-profile crime victims, Tory prime minister David Cameron set up the Leveson Inquiry to take apart the entire 'culture, ethics and practice' of the British media and propose a tough new system of regulation to help sanitise what many in high places look down upon as the 'gutter press'.

Lord Justice Leveson's final report in late 2012 called for (alongside other punitive measures) a new regulator backed by law to police the press. Shortly afterwards the leaders of Britain's major political parties stitched up a late-night deal over pizza with Hacked Off, the lobby group for state regulation fronted by celebrities such as Hugh Grant, to create a new system of press regulation. It would be underpinned by Royal Charter and overseen by Her Majesty's Most Honourable Privy Council, an ancient secretive group of senior politicians. This suitably medieval-sounding instrument was the first attempt at state-backed policing of press freedom in Britain since the Crown's licensing of all publications lapsed in 1695. The twenty-first-century press, unsurprisingly, failed to line up meekly to receive a right royal thrashing.

Regardless of their feelings about phone-hacking or tabloid journalism, anyone with a liberal mindset or a liberty-loving bone in their body should surely have risen up against this attempt to police what can be published and read, and declared that the freedom of the press is the pulse of a free society. Or as that old freedom-lover Karl Marx put it more than 150 years earlier, that 'The free press is the ubiquitous vigilant eye of a people's soul, the embodiment of a people's faith in itself'.[7] That was not quite what happened, however. Instead, many of the UK's most prominent liberals took up the cudgels in support of the Royal Charter and against excessive press freedom.

Soon after Hacked Off issued a public demand for the press to bend the knee and submit to being regulated by Royal Charter, it was able to boast that this illiberal demand had been signed by more than 200 of the UK's 'leading cultural figures'.

The list of those 200-plus prominent signatories read like a who's who of the supposedly enlightened world of arts and culture, science and literature, even including some prominent journalists. It was as if the liberal UK had signed its own death warrant.[8]

One group of signatories which caught my eye included all of the surviving members of Monty Python, then preparing for their big live comeback shows on the London stage. This was a surreal turnaround of the type which bores of a certain age (my age, sadly) might once have called 'Pythonesque'.

Thirty-five years before, the Pythons had to resist a public crusade led by Mary Whitehouse – Britain's most prominent 1970s prude – Christian bishops and Tory councillors to have their movie masterwork, *Monty Python's Life of Brian*, banned from cinemas as blasphemous. Having seen off the old forces of censorship back then, the Pythons and their successors now appeared to have effectively switched sides and joined a secular crusade for less press freedom. The jokes and sketches in their revival show might have remained the same, but the world outside had clearly changed. The excoriatingly funny anti-censorship campaigners of yesteryear (and their younger duller imitators) have become the po-faced pro-regulation prigs of our times. It might seem reasonable to conclude that open-minded liberalism is a dead parrot – not just resting and definitely not 'pinin' for the fjords', and that a new breed of 'illiberal liberalism' now rules the roost.

One of the important gains of the Enlightenment was the drawing of a firm line between the private and public spheres of life. The newly independent autonomous individual would have a public voice, and a private space in which to think and speak, free from the watchful eye of any intolerant inquisitor.

That line is now being seriously blurred. There is no place to hide from the silent war on free speech on either side of the Atlantic – even, it seems, inside your own mind.

We have witnessed a stream of scandals in the US and the UK where celebrities, sportsmen and other public figures have been pilloried and punished after revelations about the contents of their private emails, texts and phone messages led to allegations of 'secret' racism, sexism or homophobia.

It has long been accepted that there is a difference between what people think and say in private and their public statements. The notion of interrogating a person's private thoughts at the point of a hot poker went out with the Inquisition. As the seventeenth-century pioneer of English law Sir Edward Coke made clear, in modern civilised society: 'No man, ecclesiastical or temporal, should be examined upon the secret thoughts of his heart.'⁹ And a good thing too. Many of us are quite capable of ranting or ridiculing away in private to an extent we would never dream of doing in public. As the English philosopher Thomas Hobbes understood, unlike our public speech, 'The secret thoughts of a man run over all things, holy, profane, clean, obscene, grave and light, without shame, or blame.'¹⁰

No longer, it seems. Shaming and blaming men for their 'secret thoughts' is now apparently back in style. In recent years the distinction between the public and the private has become as blurred as a muddy touchline. Our voyeuristic political and media class increasingly demands that we be made accountable for what we do in private. Meanwhile exhibitionist public figures have turned their private lives into a profession.

The result of fudging the line between private and public is disastrous for freedom of thought and speech.

After basketball team owner Donald Stirling was accused of racism and drummed out of the sport over words he used in a private phone call, novelist Joyce Carol Oates felt moved to write an article headed 'End of Free Speech in America', in which she asserted the basic truth that in a democratic society we should be free to 'say anything in private, no matter how stupid, cruel, self-serving or plain wrong, and not be criminalised'. It is a dark sign of the times that those sensible words could themselves now seem shocking to many.[11]

The implications of where this ends are starker still. *Spiked* editor Brendan O'Neill wrote of the 'new inquisition' into men's private thoughts mounted in these cases that: 'There is surely only one solution to the alleged scourge of people saying bad things in private – put a telescreen in every home to capture our banter and alert the morality police to the utterance of dark or daft thoughts.'[12]

The dangerous trend towards policing private words and thoughts brings to mind the all-seeing telescreens, Thought Police and thoughtcrime from George Orwell's *Nineteen Eighty-Four*. One element of Big Brother's system of surveillance is that people are encouraged to spy on one another and inform on what their colleagues, neighbours and even their parents say and do in private.

The purpose of Orwell's Thought Police is not simply to punish those found guilty of mentally straying from the correct state diktat. It is also to encourage the rest to practise 'crimestop' – described by Big Brother's public enemy number one, Emmanuel Goldstein, as 'the faculty of stopping short, as though by instinct, at the threshold of any dangerous thought … Crimestop, in short, means protective stupidity'.[13]

Thanks, but some of us would rather take the risk of living in a relatively free world where there might be dodgy private texts lurking on somebody's smartphone, rather than one where everybody's unedited inner thoughts can be laid bare and we are kept safe in a blanket of collective 'protective stupidity'. The stymying of new ideas and stagnation of discussion and debates are just two casualties of the silent war on free speech.

It is almost 350 years since Spinoza declared that 'In a free state, every man may think what he likes and say what he thinks.' In our twenty-first-century free states, many would find his straightforward case for freedom as unpalatable as did the Jewish elders of seventeenth-century Amsterdam, who banned him from the synagogue and cursed him to damnation as a heretic. As an online mob of heretic-hunters might tweet Spinoza today, 'Think what you like and say what you think? WTF? You-Can't-Say-THAT!'

3

A short history of free-speech heretics

Free speech was not a gift from the gods or a natural right that grows on trees. Like any freedom worth having, it often had to be taken at the point of a sword as well as a pen.

That heroes of history won a degree of freedom not only to think in private but to speak as they saw fit is a victory still to be admired. But free speech is not a prize to be gained once and then taken for granted, a trophy stuck on a shelf gathering dust. Down the centuries the right to freedom of expression has had to be defended, fought for and advanced over and again, against new enemies and fresh arguments. It is worthwhile reminding ourselves how hard-won the liberties we often take too lightly today were.

This point is of more than historical interest. If freedom of expression did not always exist and had to be created by humanity, it follows that that right need not automatically exist for ever. Free speech can also be destroyed or at least redefined out of existence if we allow it.

Free speech, understood as the ability to openly express an opinion, take part in public debate and criticise those in authority, is not nearly as old in the West as some might imagine. The year 2015 marked the 800th anniversary of the sealing of England's Magna Carta, an historic document through which a collection of barons and bishops forced King John to concede for the first time certain legal rights to 'free men', including the right to trial by a jury of their peers. For establishing the idea that there were limits to the power of the Crown, the Magna Carta should rightly be celebrated as creating a prototype for liberty in the Anglo-American world, laying what one legal authority called 'the foundation for the freedom of the individual against the arbitrary power of the despot'.[1] Yet the historic Magna Carta, which establishes such important foundations of our civilisation as the standard measure of a pint of ale, makes no mention of freedom of speech. That was hardly surprising. Such a concept would have been meaningless for the mass of people in the England of 1215, among the most advanced nations of its medieval age.

In feudal society the natural order of things, accepted as God-given, was that peasants were in bondage to the lords, and did their bidding.

The one 'right' which mattered most until a few hundred years ago was the divine right of kings to rule. It was captured in the English Crown's royal motto 'Dieu et Mon Droit' – 'God and My Right'. The double meaning of 'right' is deliberate. The king ruled in theory by divine right, having been placed on the throne by the grace of God. In practice, he ruled by the exercise of 'my right' – the power of his sword-wielding right arm and the forces it commanded. Anybody who challenged that right, by word or deed, could expect to feel the force of it. (The same royal motto of state power still adorns British courts and official buildings, in case any of us upstarts start to imagine we might be free citizens rather than subjects of the Crown.)

Matters of English state were legitimately to be discussed only by the king and his courtiers, quite possibly in Norman French. Other laws enforced by the Crown and the Church ruled that matters of faith were officially to be read and spoken of only by the priesthood, in Latin. Anything else could be deemed heresy, potentially punishable by death. The political principle of free speech could not take hold in England or Europe until humanity moved history on, the notion of individual rights gained currency and people began to question the absolute power of Crown and Church.

The first printing press was introduced to England by William Caxton in 1476. The response of successive English monarchs to this miracle of the modern age (apart from an impulse to smash the infernal machine) was to control it. They imposed a system of Crown licensing under which nothing could legally be published except with the permission of the Star Chamber, a secret court of privy councillors and judges, and any criticism of the Crown could be branded treason or seditious libel.

In 1579, the Puritan John Stubbs had his writing hand publicly severed with a cleaver in Westminster marketplace for publishing a pamphlet criticising the proposed marriage of Queen Elizabeth I to a French Catholic duke. In 1637 another Puritan author, William Prynne, had his ears cut off for writing pamphlets attacking the religious policies of King Charles I's regime; Prynne was also branded on both cheeks with 'SL' for Seditious Libeller. Even as late as 1663 John Twyn was hanged, drawn and quartered at Tyburn in London – now Marble Arch – under the recently restored King Charles II, having been found guilty of high treason for printing – not writing – a 'seditious, poisonous and scandalous book' justifying the people's right to rebel against injustice.[2]

Intolerance remained a core 'value' of Western culture until the dawn of modernity. As late as 1691, the French Catholic theologian Jacques-Bénigne Bossuet could boast that: 'I have the right to persecute you because I am right and you are wrong.'[3] No nonsense about everybody being 'entitled to their opinion' there. With the ruling elites declaring their 'right to persecute' anybody whose beliefs strayed from the official line, notions of free speech were not to be tolerated.

* * *

The phrase 'freedom of speech' first appeared in English writing just less than 400 years ago, coined by the famous jurist Sir Edward Coke in his *Institutes of the Lawes of England* (first published in 1628), which laid the foundations of England's common law. It was in the seventeenth-century age of Enlightenment that the growing belief in the freedom of the individual made free speech both necessary and desirable. Even then King James I was at pains to make clear to members of parliament that 'freedome of speech ... are no Theames, or subjects fit for vulgar persons' such as MPs 'or common meetings' such as the House of Commons.[4]

Not too long after that, however, freedom of speech and of the press burst out as a burning political issue in the struggles between king, Church and parliament in the run-up to the English Revolution (often called the civil war, sometimes by those who still wish to pretend that respectable old England could never have had a bloody revolution or beheaded the king). That fire was to burn across the Atlantic, where the demand for freedom of speech and of the press would be at the heart of the American Revolution and the constitution of the new republic.

But what about the ancient Greeks? They are famous for practising free speech in their assemblies and auditoriums, a couple of thousand years before Sir Edward Coke came up with the phrase in English or the Founding Fathers wrote the First Amendment. A glance back at the Greek experience throws some revealing light on free speech in the modern age.

Freedom of speech – or *parrhesia* as they called it – did prevail in the civilised society of ancient Athens – at least for the privileged minority of full male citizens, if not for their slaves and certainly not for their womenfolk. Like much else discovered or invented by ancient civilisations, from science to sewers, the concept of free speech in society disappeared in Europe's Dark Ages before being reinvented once more in the modern world.

The Athens experience did help to mark out the field for the conflicts over free speech in the modern era. Most notably with the trial and execution of the greatest of philosophers, Socrates, who was put to death at the age of seventy for talking out of turn. Scholars have long asked how the pure democracy of Greece, founded upon a commitment to free speech among its citizens, could have executed the wisest of men as a criminal purely for what he thought and said.

The short answer is apparently that Socrates 'just went too far' in exercising his freedom of speech.[5] He was the philosopher who questioned everything, often to the discomfort of his fellow citizens, and refused to be bound by the sacred traditions or deities of Athens society. The formal charges against Socrates accused him of 'not believing in the gods that the city believes in' – heresy. Nor did Socrates believe in restraining his speech in line with the Athenian tradition of Aidos – respect, modesty or shame. He was, literally, shameless, even stripping naked to speak before his accusers to symbolise that everything must be out in the open. And the naked philosopher made clear to the Athenian court that even if they voted to spare him, he would not change, but would continue saying the unsayable and asking the forbidden questions. The jurors in the tribunal voted 280–221 for his conviction.

The trial and execution of Socrates shows that free speech can always be a dangerous and contentious thing. Many who think they believe absolutely in that principle will recoil when confronted with free speech bare-arsed and red in tooth and claw. So it could be that, in the end, as one expert study has it, '[w]hen Socrates practises *parrhesia* as the Athenians understood it, the bold affirmation and shameless articulation of what one believes to be true, the Athenians vote to execute him'.[6] How much more horrifying real free speech must seem to many who claim to support it in our timid society today.

Socrates posed the question that, for all the changes down the centuries, still stands as a central issue in the free-speech wars:

should there be a right to be a heretic? Heresy is often at the heart of struggles over free speech. What changes is what society might consider to be heresy at different stages in history.

Heresy is defined as a belief contrary to orthodox religious opinion; or in non-religious terms, an opinion profoundly at odds with what is generally accepted. An early Christian leader defined his own views as 'orthodox', from the Greek for 'right belief'. The views of his opponents he branded as heresy – from the Greek for 'choice of belief'.

The thing that has always got you branded a heretic is making an intellectual choice. Heresy is the desire to choose what you believe in and to dissent from the authoritative dogma of the day. What better case for freedom of speech could there be than that?

Those called heretics of one stripe or another have often been the heroes, the whipping boys and the *causes célèbres* in the historic struggle for freedom of speech. From the trial of Socrates to today, the big battles have been about the right to go against the grain, dissent from respectable opinion and question the unquestionable. What we might call the Right to be Offensive.

In the first wave of the modern free-speech wars in England, those demanding free speech were religious heretics. The Puritans and other advocates of the new Protestant thought wanted the right to break ranks with the ruling Church of Rome and to preach and worship in their own way. At the heart of their heretical demand was the wish to have a Bible printed in their own English language. The punishment for such heresy was for not only the book, but also the printer, to be burned at the stake. Despite the ban, William Tyndale famously printed an English version of the New Testament in Germany in 1526 and smuggled it into England. Tyndale was eventually executed by strangulation and then burned at the stake for the crime of heresy in 1536. Just three years after he was executed, Henry VIII – having by now split from Rome and founded the Church of England – gave approval for an English text, the Great Bible, based on Tyndale's translation, to be printed and made available to every church. Yesterday's blasphemous heresy had become today's orthodox religious belief.

The role of religious heretics in demanding free speech is worth remembering, when religion is often seen purely as a force for reaction and repression. Since these religious heretics came up against the censorious power of the central authority, their demands soon melded into a rising political clamour for the freedom of the press.

As the English civil war broke out between the king and parliament, John Milton published his plea for unlicensed printing in 1644, the *Areopagitica*, asking parliament to 'Give me the liberty to know, to utter, and to argue freely according to conscience, above all liberties.'[7] Milton was equally adamant that those who published blasphemy should still be punished after the event. Nor did he wish the liberty to 'utter and argue freely' to be extended to those devilish Papists or non-believers. Tolerance has always been a difficult principle to uphold in practice.

The turmoil of the English Revolution, when the king was overthrown and executed in 1649 and the 'order of the world' turned on its head, brought new voices from below into public life for the first time. The radical Levellers movement formulated its own demands for more far-reaching changes in society, not least in relation to freedom of speech and of the press. Leveller John Lilburne called for an end to state licensing of the press as 'expressly opposed and dangerous to the liberties of the people'.

The English monarchy was restored in 1660, and whatever gains for free speech had been made were soon buried again under a new system of Crown licensing of the printing press. But as the 'Glorious Revolution' replaced the autocratic Catholic King James II with the Protestant William and Mary, parliament passed a Bill of Rights in 1689. This wrote freedom of speech and debate into English law, at least for those 'vulgar persons' the members of parliament and their 'common meetings' in Westminster. It was a sign of how important the rise of free speech would be in the emerging struggle for democracy on both sides of the Atlantic that free speech should first be enshrined in law in relation to parliament – however limited both that freedom and democratic government were at first. By 1695, the system of Crown licensing of the press finally ended, and the news-sheet-reading society of the London coffee houses started to develop more liberal attitudes. The fight for freedom of speech and of the press, however, was just beginning.

In the 1760s, the English free-speech wars were carried forward by one of my favourite heretical heroes, John Wilkes – maverick journalist, printer, member of parliament and Lord Mayor of London, and a pioneer of the fight for liberty and democracy. At a time when any criticism of the Crown and its ministers could still get you locked up for seditious libel, Wilkes published a scandal-mongering newspaper, *The North Briton*, that ridiculed the royal court and its pet politicians – often suggesting, for example, that the king's mother was intimate with the prime minister – and declared on its front page that 'the liberty of the press' was 'the birthright of every Briton'.

For publishing what the authorities deemed heresy, Wilkes was convicted of both seditious libel and blasphemous libel, sent to the Tower of London, imprisoned for almost two years, declared an outlaw, expelled from parliament and then barred from returning, despite winning four elections. In the course of these personal struggles Wilkes helped win hard-fought victories for liberty. He effectively ended the British state's use of arbitrary 'general warrants' to arrest political opponents, established the right of English electors to choose their MP, and won the vital freedom of newspapers to report what the country's rulers said and did behind the doors of parliament.

Wilkes the Georgian gentleman heretic was one of the earliest examples of a people's champion, a popular figure in a way that writers or politicians could only dream of being today. The cry of 'Wilkes and Liberty!' resounded through the streets of London, often accompanied by the sounds of that pre-democratic expression of the people's will, the riot. When the fight for the right to report what was said in parliament reached its climax in 1771, and Wilkes's allies arrived at Westminster to be sent to the Tower, a reported 50,000 Londoners laid siege to parliament in their defence and came close to lynching the prime minister, Lord North. As the *Middlesex Journal* reported these riotous scenes: 'Lord North's chariot glasses were broken to pieces, as was the carriage soon afterwards, by which he received a wound, and was exceedingly terrified. The populace also took off his hat and cut it into pieces, and he narrowly escaped with his life.'[8]

The Wilkes riots left the British ruling class exceedingly terrified of a populace now demanding liberty and the freedom of the press. Yet the figure at the centre of this crisis was hardly a righteous crusader for high principles or squeaky-clean campaigner for human rights. John Wilkes was no Angelina Jolie. He was a notorious rake, a scoundrel, a womanising drunkard, gambler and debtor. He once described his journalistic method thus: 'Give me a grain of truth and I will mix it up with a great mass of falsehood so that no chemist will ever be able to separate them.'[9] His publications, which became *causes célèbres* in the fight for press freedom, mixed scurrilous scandal with downright filth. At the same time as Wilkes was convicted of seditious libel by the House of Commons for criticising the king, he was also found guilty of obscene libel by the House of Lords for publishing pornographic poetry.

Yet Wilkes the heretic and his ignoble publications helped to change the course of political history and struck a major blow for press freedom. To my mind John Wilkes the scoundrel and publisher of porn was far more of a moral force for good than any high-handed attempt to limit people's freedom of speech 'for their own good'. His story is a reminder that in the real world, freedom is less an abstract principle than a messy and sometimes bloody business, and that high-minded notions of liberty can be deployed for base aims, too. That does not alter the need to defend the principle of free speech, regardless of what we might think of its specific content, and the rights of the heretical heroes who fight for it, even if, like Wilkes, they have feet caked in clay.

The ideas of liberty pioneered by English radicals and revolutionaries such as Milton, Wilkes, Tom Paine and the two newspaper essayists who wrote as 'Cato' helped to inspire the revolutions that swept first America and then France at the end of the eighteenth century. These republican uprisings were to take the concept of free speech some way beyond its English origins.

By the 1770s, heretics who rejected the divine right of the English king to control their lives became the leaders of the American Revolution. Looking back on these momentous events later, the second US president John Adams reflected that the war for American independence which started in 1775 was not the real revolution. That, said Adams, had been the earlier revolution in the hearts and minds of the people, the spark for which had been the pamphlets and newspapers 'by which the public opinion was enlightened and informed'.[10] Freedom of expression had proved the catalyst for the creation of a free nation.

Little wonder, then, that after independence was won the First Amendment enshrined that freedom in the new US Constitution in 1791, establishing that: 'Congress shall make no law respecting an establishment of religion, or prohibiting the free exercise thereof; or abridging the freedom of speech, or of the press; or the right of the people peaceably to assemble, and to petition the Government for a redress of grievances.' Two years earlier, in 1789, the revolutionary French National Assembly had passed the declaration that: 'The free communication of thought and opinion is one of the most precious rights of man; every citizen may therefore speak, write and print freely' in the new French republic.

It might seem that the fight for freedom of speech as a universal right had been won in parts of the West, the issue settled. But history suggests that is never true – even in America. A few years after the First Amendment was passed, it was effectively bypassed by laws that sought to criminalise criticism of the US government.

The commitment of the Founding Fathers to freedom of speech was not necessarily as deep or as wide as might be assumed. Thomas Jefferson and the other Founding Fathers took their lead from the restricted form of free speech written into English law; they had, says one critical historian, 'an unbridled passion for a bridled liberty of speech'.[11]

The question of how tight that bridle should fit was soon tested, with the passage of the Aliens and Sedition laws in 1798. Not for the last time, the US government used a foreign threat, real or imagined, to justify restricting liberties at home: in this case the threat from 'Wild Irishmen' and French 'Jacobins'. The Sedition Act made it a serious offence, punishable by fines, prison and even deportation, to utter or write words which might 'defame' the US president, government or Congress, bring them into 'contempt or disrepute', or 'excite against them ... the hatred of the good people of the United States'. In short, it potentially became a crime to criticise the American government. The oppressive old English laws of seditious libel had effectively been transported to the new America, the First Amendment notwithstanding.

It was when faced with the threat of being branded seditious – that is, being cast in the role of heretics – that the opposition became First Amendment fundamentalists. James Madison now argued that the American system of government was different from the British, resting as it did on the sovereignty of the people rather than of parliament. Therefore 'a different degree of freedom in the use of the press' was required. That freedom must be extended beyond 'an exemption from previous restraint, to an exemption from subsequent penalties also'.[12] In other words Americans must have the right not only to speak and publish freely, but to be free from the threat of being punished by the government afterwards. The Sedition Act lapsed, Madison was elected fourth president of the United States in 1809, and free speech took another unsteady step forward.

The story of the First Amendment and the Sedition Act is a tale that reveals how even in the heart of the land of the free, public freedom of speech has never been a right that can safely be taken for granted for long.

Back in Britain in the early nineteenth century, freedom of speech and of the press became central issues for the Chartists and others campaigning for a democratic system of government and the extension of the vote.

Even after state licensing of the press had ended, governments imposed a stamp tax on newspapers to try to price the growing radical press out of the reach of working people. These penalties were increased after the infamous 1819 Peterloo Massacre in Manchester, when cavalry troops charged a mass rally for parliamentary reform (the booming industrial city still had no MPs to represent it), leaving an estimated 15 dead and up to 500 injured.

The government of Lord Castlereagh moved quickly, not to reform the system but to repress the protest movement and the free press. One new law increased the maximum penalty for writing or publishing 'blasphemous and seditious libels' against the religious and political authorities to fourteen years' transportation – banishment from Britain to a penal colony. Another extended the stamp tax for the first time to publications carrying political opinions. This became known contemptuously as the 'tax on knowledge'. Many radicals refused to pay it and went to jail for editing, writing or simply selling heretical newspapers. These heretics played a key role in forcing greater democracy on the 'Mother of Parliaments'.

Elsewhere in Europe, too, the radical movements that ignited the democratic revolutions of 1848 across the continent put their right to speak out against the status quo at the forefront of their demands. Karl Marx, revolutionary author of the *Communist Manifesto* and *Capital*, is often thought of as an enemy of freedom, thanks to the association of his name with the repressive system of the Stalinist Soviet Union. Less well known is that the first articles the young Marx published in a German newspaper in 1842 were a series of essays 'On Freedom of the Press', fiercely attacking Prussian state censorship and insisting that 'lack of freedom is the real mortal danger for mankind'.[13]

The nineteenth-century case for free speech took another leap forward with the publication of John Stuart Mill's *On Liberty* in 1859. Mill made an uncompromising case for individual freedom of speech as a social good, and the importance of allowing the heretical voice to test the accepted truths and values of society:

> If all mankind minus one were of one opinion, and only one person were of the contrary opinion, mankind would be no more justified in silencing that one person, than he, if he had the power, would be justified in silencing mankind ... If the opinion is right, they are deprived of the opportunity of exchanging error for truth; if wrong, they lose, what is almost as great a benefit, the clearer perception and livelier impression of truth, produced by its collision with error.[14]

Mill's message was far from universally accepted, however, even in the high seats of English learning. In that same year of 1859, Charles Darwin finally published his masterwork outlining the theory of evolution, *On the Origin of Species*. The blasphemous book was soon banned from the library of Trinity College, Cambridge, the university where Darwin had been a student.

In mid-nineteenth-century America, too, free speech was still a battleground, nowhere more so than in the struggle over slavery. Pro-slavery forces outlawed criticism of slavery in southern states, and passed 'gag rules' at federal level to prevent anti-slavery petitions being discussed in Congress, creating what one study calls 'the Southern blockade against free speech about slavery'.[15]

By the twentieth century, one might imagine that the idea of heretic-hunting and damning blasphemers was well past its use-by date in the democratic West. Yet there were still new challenges to face and battles to be fought for free speech – and not just against Nazi Germany or Stalin's Soviet Union, either. In the 'American century', it is no surprise that the US should have become a key battleground in the free-speech wars. Time and again, it was those seeking to change society who found themselves cast in the role of heretic and witch-hunted for their views.

Between the two world wars the US Supreme Court became the scene of several major cases – remarkably, the first ones it had ever heard concerning the First Amendment – that set new benchmarks in the legal battle to defend and extend free speech. We need not wade through the legal details here. Some cases were won, some lost, notably during the 'Red Scare' crackdown on political radicals after the First World War (the Supreme Court's famous ruling regarding shouting fire in a theatre is discussed later). But they helped eventually to broaden the legal definition of free speech under the First Amendment. And none of those court cases was a narrow legal affair. Most were about political heretics engaged in political struggle in wider American society, attempting to challenge the mainstream consensus and force the state to acknowledge their free-speech rights, be they anti-war agitators, religious pacifists, anarchists, socialists, anti-Semites or Communists.

In the Cold War decades after the Second World War, an icy front of anti-Communist laws sought to freeze free speech in America, with the complicity of the Supreme Court. Then, in the liberalising atmosphere of the 1960s, two challenges from heretical views at either end of the political spectrum finally broke further new ground in building the 'bulwark' of free speech in America.

In the 1964 case of *New York Times Co v. Sullivan*, the Supreme Court found for the newspaper against L. B. Sullivan, the public safety commissioner in Montgomery, who claimed that he had been libelled in an advertisement placed by the black civil rights movement. Sullivan had been awarded half a million dollars by state courts. The US Supreme Court judges ruled, however, that the First Amendment meant it should not be an offence to criticise or defame public officials, even if the criticism contained honest mistakes, unless publication was motivated by malice. As the ruling put it: '[D]ebate on public issues should be uninhibited, robust and wide open', which 'may well include vehement, caustic, and sometimes unpleasantly sharp attacks on government and public officials'.

This 1964 decision, legal observers have since noted, finally removed the ancient threat of being prosecuted for 'seditious libel' from over the heads of US heretics who criticised the authorities.[16]

Five years later in 1969, a political heretic from the other end of the spectrum helped push back the barriers further still. In *Brandenburg v. Ohio* the Supreme Court reversed the conviction of a Ku Klux Klan leader who had denounced Jews and black people at a rally. The judges ruled that simply holding or expressing hateful or inflammatory views would no longer be sufficient to break the law. Instead, under the First Amendment, a speaker would be protected except if his words were intended towards 'inciting or producing imminent lawless action' and also 'likely to produce such action'.[17] Establishing the right of the KKK to spout its bile may not seem like a particularly famous victory for freedom today, but in drawing a firm line between hateful words and deeds, and affirming that the holding of views that many found repugnant could not in itself be considered a crime, it laid a firmer foundation for free speech in America as an indivisible and universal right.

Back in the slightly more stultified British society, meanwhile, the post-war era was also marked by some set-piece legal battles over freedom of expression between the conventional forces of reaction and the new cultural heretics.

In 1960 the failed prosecution of Penguin Books under new obscenity laws, for publishing D. H. Lawrence's sexually explicit novel *Lady Chatterley's Lover*, ushered in an era of more liberalised publishing. In 1971, however, three editors of the 'alternative' magazine *Oz* who had wrongly assumed that the battle was over were found guilty of obscenity for their infamous Schoolkids edition, which included a cartoon of Rupert the Bear having sex. For this blasphemy against St Rupert of Nutwood, they were sentenced to up to fifteen months in prison, though the convictions were quashed on appeal.

Then in 1977, Christian censorship crusader Mary Whitehouse successfully brought a private prosecution for blasphemy against *Gay News*, over a poem in which a Roman centurion describes having sex with a gay Jesus after his crucifixion. *Gay News* was fined £1,000, which increased to £10,000 with court costs, and its publisher, Denis Lemon, was given a suspended jail sentence.

These were the last throws of the old censorious order. There would be no more trials for obscene publications or blasphemous libels in Britain. The offences of blasphemy and blasphemous libel were finally abolished by the New Labour government in 2008. It seemed that the West's cultural heretics, like the political ones before them, had come in from the cold.

That was only the end of the fight for free speech against its old enemies. New ones would soon emerge. In recent times the offences of heresy and blasphemy have simply been redefined again in Anglo-American culture and society. Now we have new heretics, new blasphemies and new orthodoxies.

Hate-speech laws in the UK have even reintroduced a form of blasphemy-lite onto the statute books, effectively making crimes of racial and religious hatred and homophobia. And there are many new informal rules about things that cannot be said, heresies that should not be spread. The fact that the proponents of the old orthodoxies can now find themselves in the dock – like the

Christian and Muslim preachers convicted in UK courts for preaching words deemed homophobic – might raise a wry smile in some quarters. But heresy-hunting is still a threat to free speech, no matter who is on the receiving end, be they religious bigot or cartoon bear-baiter.

Today the biggest threat comes not from official bans and censorship imposed in the name of central authority and intolerance, but from unofficial censorship and an atmosphere of conformism justified in the language of protecting rights and diversity. That often makes the danger more covert and trickier to oppose. But the lesson of history is that defending free speech means standing up for the rights of heretics, no matter what we might think of them or how hard that might seem in the here and now.

Five good excuses for restricting free speech – and why they're all wrong

4

'... but words will *always* hurt me'

The prosecution alleges that some speech, particularly 'hate speech', is just too hurtful and offensive to be allowed to go free.

The traditional playground chant that 'Sticks and stones may break my bones/But words will never hurt me' must now be one of the most unfashionable of old-fashioned wisdoms. These days it is treated with about the same level of popular respect as the Book of Leviticus in the Old Testament (the one that says God wants us to sacrifice animals and slaughter homosexuals).

The consensus now is that words hurt, by causing harm and offence. Indeed it is often argued that hurtful words cause emotional wounds and psychological scars that are worse and more lasting than the external marks of physical abuse. As the British celebrity intellectual Stephen Fry says, 'Sticks and stones may break my bones, but words will *always* hurt me.'[1]

The old rhyme, like many things children might say, is not strictly true. In the real grown-up world words can certainly hurt in their way, and not only the abusive ones; there are few things more painful than an unwanted 'Goodbye'.

But unlike Leviticus, the past wisdom of the playground still has something important to teach us. There is indeed a difference between sticks and stones and words, between speech and deeds, between offensive language and physical violence. The protection of the law must be upheld for those who are assaulted or oppressed (although paper 'rights' won't stop punches or bullets in the first place). But there can be no right not to be offended. Or to put it another way, anyone is entitled to take offence at anything said by anybody else. But taking offence does not give them any right to take away somebody else's freedom of speech.

Instead of free speech, however, the demand from radical campaigners these days is more often for freedom from offensive words.

Measures imposed to deal with the scourge of offensive words range from formal laws against 'hate speech' in the UK and Europe, through 'No platform' policies and bans on US and UK university campuses, to the informal but pervasive conformism of the You-Can't-Say-That culture across the Anglo-American world.

We are not talking here primarily about the use of abusive language, but the expression of offensive opinions. Barely a day now seems to pass without another news story about somebody claiming to have been offended or harmed by what somebody else has said, and demanding that something must be done about it. Jokes are a constant target of the offence-takers. Postings found to be offensive on social media are likely not only to be ripped apart by an online lynch mob, but also reported to the police. And British police commanders, who seem more comfortable policing the tweets than the streets, have made it clear that they want to crack down not just on criminal offences online, but offensive words and opinions also.

From the point of view of the reverse-Voltaires, the beauty of this line of attack is that offensiveness is in the eye of the offended beholder. Whether or not you consider any speech offensive is an entirely subjective judgement, based on your feelings. Nobody else can disagree and tell you that you are not offended. For you to say 'You have offended me' thus becomes an apparently unanswerable argument for censorship. Determined to prevent and punish the expression of anything with which they disagree, the new censors have homed in on offensive speech as an easy target against which to assert their moral superiority.

The crusade against offensive speech now extends from the low comedy of social media 'banter' to high-powered political debates. As Richard King, author of *On Offence*, observes, going on the offensive has been part of political struggles since ancient times, as 'the word offend derives from *offendere*, a Latin word meaning "to strike against"'. Offensive arguments that strike against your opponents have long been the normal ammunition of a political fight. Things are different in politics today, however: '[I]n the twenty-first century, it isn't only offence, but also the *taking* of offence that is weaponised – that is, used to strike against opponents.'[2]

Taking offence at the other side's argument has itself become an easy knee-jerk intervention, without the awkward necessity of having to come up with an argument of your own. To claim that you feel offended by something your opponent says has become a short-cut to winning – or at least, ending – a political debate, regardless of the relative merits of debaters' points.

This habit of offence-taking hypersensitivity has become so normalised it might be hard to remember what a change it represents from the past. The sticks-and-stones rhyme captured the attitude that most adults once wanted to impart to their children: that in growing up in a free society you had to learn to cope with the rough and tumble of other people's words and opinions without shedding too many tears.

Once upon a time, the taking and giving of offence was seen as an inevitable part of a full life. Back in 1838, the Scottish historian and philosopher Thomas Carlyle published a short biography of the novelist Sir Walter Scott. Discussing how to present the life of a great man without making him appear too much like a plaster saint, Carlyle captured an important truth about life in a free and dynamic society when he wrote that: 'No man lives without jostling or being jostled; in all ways he has to elbow himself through the world, giving and receiving offence. His life is like a battle, insofar as it is an entity at all.'[3]

Elbowing through the world, giving and receiving offence, treating life like a battle? Today the cry would surely go up (probably via Twitter) to lock that man away, or at the very least take away his smartphone privileges.

The historic shift in attitude is illustrated by the attempt to rewrite one of the classical cases for free speech, J. S. Mill's *On Liberty* (1859), into a modern-day demand for restricting hate speech. Mill's essay was a ground-breaking argument for freedom. He argued that an individual should be sovereign over himself, and could not be compelled to do or say anything he did not want to even if it was deemed to be for his own good. The single exception to this rule, Mill allowed, was if he was harming somebody else: 'The only purpose for which power can be rightfully exercised over any member of a civilized community, against his will, is to prevent harm to others.'[4]

This subsequently became known as the harm principle. For Mill, it was almost an aside in his uncompromising defence of liberty. Yet today you could be forgiven for thinking that *On Liberty* was actually called *On Harm*, since the 'harm principle' is the only aspect of that work you are likely to hear reference to. What is more, Mill's carefully limited grounds for restraint have been expanded beyond recognition, so that 'harm' is now equated with being offended or upset by somebody else's speech. Mill's argument for free speech has been turned into its opposite. Some might call that taking liberties.

The attempt to de-normalise any speech which somebody finds offensive is having a stultifying effect on public debate, encouraging an atmosphere of tame conformism and mute self-censorship. The biggest victim is not the one who is taking offence; it is the rest of us, robbed of the opportunity for open-minded discussion and free debate that offers our best hope of getting at the truth and deciding a way forward on controversial issues.

How have we come to this state of affairs? It surely cannot simply be that more people are using more offensive forms of speech these days. What has changed is the way we respond to other people's speech, and the widespread propensity for taking offence at the drop of a disrespectful word.

It is significant in this respect that the most explosive incidents tend to be sparked by speech deemed offensive, not just to an individual, but to an entire self-defined group, be they Muslims or members of the transgender community.

The advance of the culture of offence-taking can be plotted in inverse proportion to the retreat into the politics of identity.

In recent decades Western societies have lost any powerful sense of an overarching belief system holding people together. Churches, political parties and other traditionally unifying institutions have fallen into public disrepute. The big ideologies of both left and right, which dominated Western thought for two centuries, appear exhausted and irrelevant to most people's lives. It has become commonplace for commentators to describe our societies today as atomised, individuated, a 'lonely crowd'. The angst-ridden question 'Who are we now?' forms the background to political debates such as the tortuous attempts to define the modern meaning of 'Britishness', and the endless Culture Wars in the USA.

Faced with a crisis of social cohesion and the lack of a moral consensus today, many still desperately want something to cling to that is bigger than their own selves. In search of that something, they have retreated from the failed society-wide Political (large P) projects of the recent past, into more segmented cultural and political (small p) identities. Alongside other consequences that are beyond the scope of this argument, the withdrawal into identity politics has had a serious impact on free speech and open debate.

A self-defined identity – whether it be as a black woman, gay man or Muslim – is seen as fixed; it is what you are, not something you are striving to be. As such it is a closed-off state, not open to question or challenge by anybody else. Moreover, since an identity is subjective – it is who you say you are – the members of an identity group assume the right to define the truth about themselves. They insist on a moral monopoly over their story. If you are not black, female or gay, you can have no say on issues which affect them.

In an inversion of the old aristocratic rule that discussing politics was the preserve of the right class of person, the suggestion now is that only the right identity groups have the right to express opinions about certain issues.

The consequences of this for freedom of speech in society have been dire. It has created a sort of privatised form of blasphemy, where it is widely accepted that intruding on the personal space of an identity group – by, for example, questioning the institution of gay marriage, or gay adoption – puts you beyond the pale. Informal censorship and self-censorship are the inevitable results of what Frank Furedi, author of *On Tolerance*, defines as 'the criminalisation of criticism'.[5]

What passes for debate today often looks more like an arms race to see who can appear most offended. Identity politics is the sphere of competitive victimhood. Identity groups draw their moral authority from claims for redress for grievances and offences against them, past and present. The insistence that you are constantly vulnerable and victimised reinforces the tendency to take offence at any opinion outside your identity's narrow worldview. Since identity is defined subjectively, it matters not what the intention of the offending speaker or writer might have been. If the identity group says it is offensive, then it automatically must be so, and demands for a withdrawal, apology and possibly compensation will follow.

If you say that you're offended, who can disagree? Nobody is allowed to say that you have not been offended (they can, of course, insist apologetically that no offence was intended, but what does that matter when your feelings decide the truth?). Once the priority of subjective feelings of offence is accepted, it becomes difficult to resist the demands for apologies and withdrawal that will soon follow. This is different from an allegation of physical assault, where objective criteria can be applied – it is not solely up to you to decide whether you have been punched or not. A personal insistence that you have been offended, however, provides a seemingly unanswerable case for demanding redress in any situation.

This subjective interpretation of events has even been written into UK law. Following the recommendations of the 1999 Macpherson Report, into the London murder of a young black man called Stephen Lawrence, criminal law has been rewritten to define a 'racist incident' as 'any incident which is perceived to be racist by the victim or any other person'. If anybody says it's racist, then officially it is. New laws against 'hate speech' in the UK and the EU have ensured that this sweeping subjective definition applies to offensive words as well as actions.

There is nothing wrong with genuinely taking offence, of course, any more than with giving it by expressing an honest opinion. But what we have here is politicised instrumental offence-taking in the age of the reverse-Voltaires. Identity activists go out looking for some speech to be offended by, and when they find it (which they always will) they demand that the speaker cease and desist. The insistence that speech must be policed to protect the hurt feelings of a few who claim to find it offensive has far wider consequences. It encroaches on the rights of us all, limiting our ability to generate much heat or light in public debates.

We might say that there is 'no right not to be offended'. But in fact many prominent offence-takers would not want any such right to be upheld anyway, if it meant they never had to hear another offensive word. Taking offence is as much a part of their lives as taking a breath. All that they ask is the right to demand redress for speech they deem offensive. They want the 'right' not to be offended only in order to protest that it has been violated.

One powerful indication of those trends is the way that laws against speech branded hateful or harmful have been introduced in the UK and the European Union. These 'hate-speech' laws truly mark the criminalisation of criticism.

The distinguishing feature of hate-speech laws is that they have managed both to restrict freedom of expression and to further swell the tendency to take offence. Well done everybody.

In the UK, the New Labour government introduced hate-speech laws via the Racial and Religious Hatred Act of 2006, amended two years later to include hatred on the grounds of sexual orientation. The EU mandated Europe-wide hate-speech laws in 2008. These laws are officially justified with high-minded talk about encouraging tolerance and equality.

Far from bringing the promised 'social peace and public order' to Europe, however, the hate-speech laws appear to have helped to inflame the tensions around 'offensive' forms of expression that erupted in the *Charlie Hebdo* massacre. It is not too hard to see why. These laws officially sanction the notion that offensive speech is a crime, and that being offended is a cause for censorious action. Hate-speech laws give the green light to anybody with a grudge who wants to outlaw or suppress opinions they find upsetting.

As one conservative American commentator put it after *Charlie Hebdo*, these laws are 'part of the problem' because they 'fan sentiments of offence' and 'give validity to expectations that speech disrespectful of Islamic symbols, practices and beliefs ought to be punished'. In 2015, the gunmen decided to cut out the middleman and 'take it upon themselves to carry this [punishment] out'.[6]

Hate-speech laws set a dangerous precedent by writing into the statute book an entirely subjectively defined offence. Few can agree on what the term 'hate speech' really means (apparently it is popular with that equally loosely defined phenomenon, the 'troll'). They only agree that they all hate any speech that criticises their culture and identity.

The consequence of all these laws is that people who have done nothing are being convicted and branded as criminals. Done nothing, that is, except express an opinion deemed insulting or offensive to somebody else's religion or identity group. Almost 250 years ago, American Founding Father Thomas Jefferson defined the classic liberal attitude to keeping the law out of religious disputes and insults, declaring that 'it does me no injury for my neighbor to say there are 20 gods or no God. It neither picks my pocket nor breaks my leg.'[7] In the civilised capitals of twenty-first-century Europe, however, it is not necessary to pick a pocket or break a leg in order to be criminalised for criticising somebody else's beliefs.

The protection which Jefferson and his peers provided for free speech under the First Amendment means that there are no hate-speech laws in America. Not yet, anyway. But opinion polls show growing support for such measures. US campuses have already effectively banned any speech which identity groups find offensive. There are those who demand that America goes much further and faster down the slippery slope.

Far from protecting public order or social peace, laws against hate speech that prevent the honest airing of controversial views are more likely merely to suppress conflicts and intensify hidden hostilities; as the British comedian Rowan Atkinson said in opposing the UK's hate-speech legislation, they can impose 'a veneer of tolerance concealing a snakepit of unaired and unchallenged views.'[8]

And it gets worse. The proliferation of 'phobias' in public discussion is one symptom of the way that criticism and questioning are being delegitimised. It is apparently no longer enough simply to say that somebody's views are offensive. The person in question must be certified as suffering from a phobia – they are homophobic, Islamophobic, transphobic, etcphobic. These shorthand labels betray a deeper prejudice. They suggest that those who hold the opinions that offend are not merely wrong-headed, but are experiencing a form of mental illness. The spread of such '-phobic' name-calling effectively turns political or cultural dissent from the mainstream into a pathology. As such, it puts an immediate end to the debate. After all, who wants to waste time having an argument with the psychiatrically disturbed? Those suffering from these phobias are not to be conversed with or treated like normal people. Instead, for the good of society they should be placed in a strait-jacket and a padded cell, figuratively if not literally.

Why do transgender activists so often seem to be in the media front line of the battles over free speech and offensiveness? Obviously they are entitled to feel offended by other people's words and to respond as they see fit. But there must be something else going on here, to explain why a relative handful of trans activists have become such a *cause célèbre* for all those who want to restrict offensive speech today.

Perhaps the clue is that to be transgender is an entirely subjective, self-defined identity. As the leading LGBT lobby GLAAD defines 'gender identity' in its media reference guide, 'For transgender people, their own internal gender identity does not match the sex they were assigned at birth.'[9] Transgender people thus insist on their right to define their own gender identity, regardless of their biology. Trans activists take great offence at those – including 'phobic' feminists – who refuse to use the term 'cis' to describe those who were born female, aka 'non-trans' women, or who use the pronoun 'he' in relation to 'trans people' who are biologically male.

The entirely subjective character of the transgender identity makes these few activists the perfect human shields behind which the reverse-Voltaires can pursue their crusade against free speech. They can decide they are women, in a triumph of personal will over physical reality. Then they insist that they have a moral monopoly over their truth, their story – and that everybody else must accept it unquestioningly. It is not necessary to insult them intentionally to cause offence. They will take exception to a factual description which fails to obey their rules. Thus to call these biological men 'he' is enough to make you an offensive, phobic bigot.

By changing the words we are allowed to use, the trans activists insist that they are altering reality. Hence they are determined to stop any 'not-trans people' saying or thinking anything about them that they don't like. It is this censorious subjectivity, this belief in a form of personalised blasphemy, that makes the transgender lobby such poster boys, or perhaps poster 'women without vaginas', for the new creed of intolerance in the name of tolerance. It is why this handful of trans activists is in the front line of the war against 'offensive' free speech. The power of veto over what others can legitimately say about them might even help to explain the appeal of adopting a trans identity to some. Just don't call them the tranny state. Or the trannyban.

What could be wrong with minorities and identity groups demanding freedom from offence? Anybody is entitled to be offended. But not to use that feeling as a weapon to curtail the rights of the rest of us.

What is really being said by these campaigns is that people can be the victims of words, in need of protection from speech. That they are objects to which things are done, rather than subjects who can shake things up and make change happen. So their interests are apparently best served by having less freedom rather than more.

This presents a striking contrast with the not-too-distant past. In times when women, black people, gays and other oppressed groups in the West faced far more abuse, discrimination and violence than today, they fought for greater freedom of expression to give them a voice. It was accepted that a precondition for fighting for equality and liberty was being able to speak, read and debate as you saw fit, regardless of how much it offended the other side. Thus freedom fighters from the Suffragettes to the Gay Liberation Movement put free speech to the fore. Their aim in speaking out was not to gain recognition as a closed, separate group with its own identity, but to win their freedom as equal citizens of a free society.

For the most accomplished argument for free speech from those fighting against oppression, we might go back further to the black

American anti-slavery campaigner – and former slave – Frederick Douglass. In 1860, faced with violent repression of debate by pro-slavery forces, Douglass wrote his famous pamphlet entitled 'A Plea for Free Speech in Boston', in which he argued:

> To suppress free speech is a double wrong. It violates the rights of the hearer as well as those of the speaker. It is just as criminal to rob a man of his right to speak and hear as it would be to rob him of his money … And until the right is accorded to the humblest as freely as to the most exalted citizen, the government of Boston is but an empty name, and its freedom a mockery. A man's right to speak does not depend upon where he was born or upon his color. The simple quality of manhood is the solid basis of the right – and there let it rest forever.[10]

If only. The former slave's appeal for free speech might sound like a foreign language to many claiming to stand for equality today.

All of these opinions were deemed highly offensive in their time, and the oppressed had to fight tooth and nail against the authorities for their right to express them. Are identity groups really so assaulted by hateful and offensive speech today that they must demand the authorities protect them from words by restricting the free speech of others? Though much has changed, to suppress free speech remains, in Douglass's words, 'a double wrong'. There is no way to emancipation through demanding bans and self-censorship.

One last thought. The right to be offensive does not impose an obligation to be offensive. And defending the uncompromised right to be offensive need not mean endorsing the way the right is exercised by others.

In fact there is generally little to celebrate in self-conscious and often self-serving acts of offensiveness. As William Hazlitt wrote, 'An honest man speaks the truth, though it may give offence, a vain man, in order that it may.'[11] We do not have to endorse those vain men – but we should defend their freedom to speak their version of the truth. And we should recognise that their token offensive gestures are a minor side effect of the far bigger problem of the culture of conformism and the war on 'offensive' free speech. Otherwise it may soon be a case of: 'When they came for the comedians and cartoonists, I did nothing because I was not a cartoonist or a comedian …'

5

'There is no right to shout "Fire!" in a crowded theatre'

The prosecution alleges that some speech is simply too dangerous and inflammatory to be allowed to go free – even under a US-style First Amendment.

There is today a flourishing market in fashionable short-hand rebukes and code words, deployed to tell somebody to shut up – 'I feel offended/That's hate speech/Check your privilege/Denier!' and so on. But the granddaddy of lines for dismissing a free-speech defence, which pre-dates those recent blow-ins and will probably still be around after they have been forgotten, is the shrill retort: 'There is no right to shout "Fire!" in a crowded theatre.'

Those who allege that some speech can simply be too dangerous to allow it to go unchecked want to silence and punish those who use inflammatory language. Rather than an assault on the troublemakers' right to free speech, we are assured, proscribing such expressions is simply an attempt to protect people and society from the consequences of dangerous talk (or lion-poking cartoons).

The top authority cited for this case against unfettered free speech is Justice Oliver Wendell Holmes of the US Supreme Court. It was Holmes who, writing the unanimous judgement back in a 1919 case, ruled that: 'The most stringent protection of free speech would not protect a man in falsely shouting fire in a theater and causing a panic.' Justice Holmes's memorable metaphor is still cited as a supposedly powerful case for dousing any speech considered inflammatory today. The abiding popularity of the fire-in-a-theatre metaphor reflects how we spend far more time discussing the need to rein in free speech than to free it.

It is worth looking a bit closer at this as a case study in how facts can be twisted, arguments turned on their heads and history rewritten, all to manufacture a legitimate-sounding excuse for hobbling free speech.

The Supreme Court case where all this began did not, of course, have anything to do with shouting 'Fire!' in a theatre or anywhere else.

In 1917, when the US joined the Allied side in the First World War, Congress passed the Conscription Act and began drafting men into the armed forces. Charles Schenck, secretary of the US Socialist Party, mailed anti-conscription leaflets to several thousand potential draftees. The self-consciously moderate leaflet – originally written in Yiddish, not English – began by citing the First Amendment to the US Constitution, which protects freedom of speech and of religion. It argued that the authorities 'violate the provisions of the United States Constitution, the Supreme Law of the Land, when they refuse to recognise your right to assert your opposition to the draft'. Schenck was charged and convicted under the wartime Espionage Act, which made it an offence to 'willfully obstruct the recruiting or enlistment service of the United States'. Although the war ended in 1918, Schenck's fight to establish his First Amendment rights to express an opinion did not. In 1919 *Schenck v. United States* reached the US Supreme Court for final judgement.

The Supreme Court judges voted unanimously to uphold his conviction, and Justice Holmes wrote the official opinion or judgement on behalf of them all. Holmes's judgement dismissed the First Amendment defence as if it was unworthy of serious consideration. Yet in so doing, he set a benchmark for the limits of free speech under the US Constitution:

> [The] question in every case is whether the words used are used in such circumstances and are of such a nature as to create a clear and present danger that they will bring about the substantive evils that Congress has a right to prevent … We admit that in many places and in ordinary times the defendants in saying all that was said in the circular would have been within their constitutional rights. But the character of every act depends upon the circumstances in which it is done. The most stringent protection of free speech would not protect a man in falsely shouting fire in a theater and causing a panic.[1]

Holmes's objection was not to the language Schenck used or even the message his anti-conscription leaflet or 'circular' conveyed. For the judge the key question was: did the words present 'a clear and present danger' of creating 'substantive evils'? That could only be answered, he said, by judging the context in which they were used. Holmes could concede that, in different circumstances, Schenck and his Socialist allies would have been within their rights to say what they did. But not when judged in the very particular context of national crisis and war. That was what his fire-in-a-theatre point was supposed to illustrate: that you could shout fire falsely to your heart's content in a field or on the beach, but it would have very different consequences in a theatre.

Justice Holmes's judgement, then, was that speech could be criminalised only in very specific, narrowly defined circumstances where it posed a 'clear and present danger'. What's wrong with that reasonable-sounding argument today?

Plenty. The old fire-in-a-theatre metaphor has been turned into a clear and present danger to freedom of speech in the here and now. Here are four reasons why it's time to put out the flame keeping that argument alive.

First, it has been distorted beyond recognition. Contrary to the common misquotation. Holmes did not say there was 'no freedom to cry "fire" in a crowded theatre'. That would have been ridiculous. What is anybody supposed to do if they spot a fire in a theatre, just exit quietly and leave the rest of the audience to roast in peace?

What Holmes said was that there was no freedom 'falsely' to cry fire. That f-word matters. It raises the question: who is to decide if the argument put forward is 'false' or not? And how, unless they are allowed to hear it in the first place? Justice Holmes assumed the Supreme Court's right, not to prevent the Socialist Party's leaflet being published, but to punish Schenck after the event. Many advocates of the fire-in-a-theatre line today go further and want to prevent the public hearing 'inflammatory' speech in the first place, and deciding for itself what might be true or false. That is prior constraint and state censorship of free speech, however you dress it up for an evening at the theatre.

This sort of misquoting of the fire-in-a-theatre is symptomatic of a wider misrepresentation. The crusaders have turned Justice Holmes's curt remark about the very specific circumstances in which he believed speech could be punished despite the First Amendment, into a general excuse for trying to outlaw or control 'dangerous' words and opinions which they simply find objectionable, whether expressed by climate-change 'deniers', 'Islamophobic' politicians, Islamist preachers or sexist comedians.

The case against shouting-fire-in-a-theatre has been expanded into a theatrical ticket for anybody who wants to impose a limit on dangerous ideas, which means ideas that they don't like. It has been twisted into an access-all-areas argument with which nobody can surely disagree. Except perhaps Justice Holmes, but fortunately for them he's not around to correct anybody.

Second, Holmes himself effectively abandoned his own words. If all of our amateur law experts are apparently so interested in spreading the wise words of Justice Oliver Wendell Holmes, then why are these students of Supreme Court history so selective about which ones they highlight?

The danger test and the fire-in-a-theatre image Justice Holmes conjured up in his Schenck judgement stand out as the occasion when he displayed a notable nervousness about free speech. In later cases – where his judgement was more considered than the brush-off he gave Schenck – the judge seemed to take a different view. He came down firmly in favour of freedom of speech even when he strongly disapproved of the sentiments expressed. Yet for some reason we don't seem to hear much about these cases outside law school seminars.

For example, ten years later, in the 1929 case of *United States v. Schwimmer*, Justice Holmes dissented from the Supreme Court's majority decision on free-speech grounds. Rosika Schwimmer was a refugee from repressive Hungary who applied to become a naturalised US citizen. In her application she admitted that, as a dedicated pacifist, she would be unable to take up arms to defend America. The majority of Supreme Court judges ruled that this meant she failed to meet the requirements of US citizenship (even though, as an elderly woman in a country that had never conscripted women or the elderly, it was an entirely hypothetical question). Writing a dissenting minority opinion on the case (which arguably reflected a majority of commentators' opinion outside the court), Justice Holmes observed that: 'Some of her answers might excite popular prejudice, but if there is any principle of the Constitution that more imperatively calls for attachment than any other it is the principle of free thought – not free thought for those who agree with us but freedom for the thought that we hate.'[2]

If you seek an historic monument to Holmes's views on freedom of expression, that is surely the line that stands the test of time. The clarion call to defend 'freedom for the thought that we hate' is crucial, not just for the US Constitution but for the foundations of any free and civilised society.

Instead, reciting the fire-in-a-theatre line has become another excuse for trying to cherry-pick who deserves to get freedom of speech.

Third, it has not been the law in the US for almost fifty years. Why do so many on both sides of the Atlantic seem keen to cite a Supreme Court case from 1919, rather than one from 1969 that superseded it? Surely it's not because they simply want to grasp at some legal straw, no matter how outdated, to give an air of authority to their thoroughly modern wish to restrain free speech?

The Supreme Court redefined the possible limits of free speech more narrowly in the 1969 case of *Brandenburg v. Ohio*. It reversed the conviction of a Ku Klux Klan leader who had spoken at a rally where armed, hooded men burned crosses and threatened 'revengeance' against 'niggers' and Jews.

The judgement in *Brandenburg* threw over the Holmes formulation from 1919 and replaced it with a freer one. From now on, in order to have your First Amendment rights restricted, the court would need to show that the words were intended to cause serious harm, and that there was an 'imminent' prospect of them doing so. Simply holding or expressing a hateful or inflammatory opinion could no longer be considered a crime, even if that opinion included the 'mere advocacy' of violence or law-breaking.

The Supreme Court judgement superseding Holmes was delivered, remember, more than forty-five years ago. Yet Holmes's creaky line is still being quoted, perhaps more than ever, to demand and justify restrictions on free speech. It has been running for even longer than *The Mousetrap* on the London stage, and its fans seem determined to stick to their dusty old script whatever the weather outside.

* * *

Fourth and finally, in any case, the fire-in-a-theatre comparison is and always was wrong. It is worth asking if Holmes had a point, anyway. Yes, his famous judgement actually set pretty narrow terms on which free speech might be abridged in very specific circumstances. But should there really be legitimate grounds to limit speech as too dangerous?

The answer is no, there shouldn't be – once we are clear what free speech means. Explicit threats against specific targets are not free speech. Neither is giving a direct order to others to commit a crime or do somebody harm. Nor, we might concede, is it freedom of expression falsely to shout you-know-what, you-know-where.

But that's why Holmes never had a case. He used a theatrical example that had nothing to do with free speech in order to attack something that definitely did – the freedom of political campaigners to criticise conscription. Whether or not there is a 'right' falsely to shout fire in a theatre, if free speech means anything there must be a right to protest against the government's war policies.

Justice Holmes's famous dictum was not about free speech at all. From today's perspective it sounds more like an issue of health and safety policy. On the other hand, firebrand speeches made by anti-war agitators, revolutionaries and even KKK racists most certainly are free-speech issues. They involve ideas, beliefs, passions and hatreds in an argument about what sort of society we want. There should never be any constraint on that sort of debate, however heated. We always need more speech rather than less to clarify the arguments and let people choose their idea of the truth.

The wish to throw a bucket of ice water on 'inflammatory' speech often reflects the prejudice that the public are mostly highly flammable blockheads, so that public opinion might be a pogrom waiting to happen at the drop of a hateful word. That is the base view of humanity that those who lazily repeat the fire-in-a-theatre line to justify restricting speech are really signing up to today.

The list of types of expression that reverse-Voltaires want to see restricted on fire-in-the-theatre grounds seems to grow longer all the time. It now includes not only Islamist preaching or Islamophobic rhetoric, but also offensive jokes, football chants, sexist/gun-glorifying gangsta rap, homophobic dancehall reggae and much more. With any of these apparently considered capable of inflaming mob violence, it seems a wonder that the streets are not constantly running with blood.

Any attempt to restrict or punish speech as incitement in a civilised society should surely be forced at the very least to pass the test set by the 1969 Brandenburg case cited above: to show that the speech was both intended to, and likely to, incite 'imminent lawless action'. Instead the tendency in the West today is to try to broaden the definition of incitement to include any 'inflammatory' words that are deemed too far beyond the pale. Broadening the legal definition of incitement risks criminalising arguments and opinions.

There is often an immediate assumption that inciting others must mean incitement to commit a crime. But the origins of the term incitement are about urging somebody forward in a particular direction, prompting them to act as you suggest. As Justice Holmes of fire-in-a-theatre fame himself put it, in one of his other less-remembered Supreme Court opinions, 'Every idea is an incitement.'[3]

Of course it is also possible to try to incite somebody to commit a crime. But we are still only talking about words, and context should be all-important in judging guilt. To express a general inflammatory attitude – for example, that the country would be better off if it could rid itself of ginger-headed people – is one thing; to urge a specific action in a particular context – 'let's get that ginger bastard over there!' – to a mob scared witless of being attacked by ginger thugs is another matter. The latter might sound like a criminal offence, the former merely an offensive opinion, and there should not be a law against it.

To what extent should a speaker be held responsible for the actions of others? A key legal consideration must be whether, in the context of the inflammatory remarks, the listener has an opportunity to reflect before acting. The 'incitees' themselves still have to choose to act on those words, and commit the offence being incited. They are not pre-programmed automatons having their buttons pushed, or actors following a script. Furthermore, since the Second World War, we have been generally reluctant to accept the excuse that somebody was 'only following orders'.

To claim that a speaker can be held directly responsible for the actions of others risks making the idea of personal responsibility meaningless. It infantilises the listeners, suggesting that they are childlike simpletons who will simply do as they are told. When I hear accusations of incitement being thrown around these days, it sometimes brings to mind the image of an exasperated mother demanding of her embarrassed son: 'Oh, little Johnny told you to do it, did he? And if Johnny "told you" to jump off a tall building, would you do that, too?'

Broadening definitions of the crime of incitement risks blurring the distinction between words and deeds, speech and action. It means blaming those who imagine an outcome for the fact that others might choose to act out their fantasies. King Henry II of England did not commit murder when he (allegedly) demanded: 'Will no one rid me of this turbulent priest?' That crime was committed by the four knights who took their king's words as a licence to assassinate Archbishop Thomas Becket in Canterbury Cathedral. Today, Henry might find himself charged with 'encouraging or assisting' an offence (since 2008 the statutory replacement of common law incitement), or at least he would if it weren't for the small matter of the British monarch still being immune from prosecution. The collapsing of aggressive words into violent deeds is bad news for freedom of thought and speech in a free society.

The UK's more recent laws creating and extending the crime of incitement to racial or religious or homophobic hatred make clear the dangerous implications of this mission creep. We may find racial or religious hatred offensive. They should no more be a criminal offence than any other opinion or emotion. Yet the offence of incitement to hatred makes it a crime to say something which might persuade others not to commit a crime but simply to think in a way deemed unacceptable in polite society.

And what about in times of war, the precise and extraordinary circumstances in which Justice Holmes imposed his rules on restricting freedom of speech? It is not hard to see how it might have been in the interests of the UK or US state to restrict freedom of speech in the midst of the national crises occasioned by the First and Second World Wars. From the point of view of defending the principles of a free society, however, some of us might think it important to advocate the right to dissent and argue for alternatives even – or especially – when democracy is on the line.

Today we are a long way from those earth-shattering world wars of the twentieth century. Yet we are witnessing the resurgence of wartime arguments about the need to control 'dangerous' speech, in relation to the conflict between Western societies and Islamist terrorism. In comparison with the powerful enemies of the past such as Nazi Germany or the Soviet Union, these nihilistic Islamists – whilst posing a mortal threat to individuals – are effectively throwing snowballs at the West's castle walls. Nevertheless the conflict with them has been used to justify new measures against 'extremist' speech – whether of the Islamophobe or Islamophile variety – from the streets of Britain to UK and US university campuses.

The attempt to extend the fire-in-a-theatre fears of the First World War to the conflict with cliques of radical Islamists today reveals the lack of faith in freedom at the heart of our societies. Are our leaders now so afraid of our own shadows, thoughts and words that they must try to restrict speech further, because they do not trust their ability to win an argument with such intellectually feeble opponents? To use the shouting-fire-in-a-theatre dictum to condemn or try to ban Islamist or anti-Islamist speech or cartoons suggests that the theatre of Western civilisation must be a crumbling edifice, if it can seriously be threatened with panic and destruction by a few shrill words from the wings.

If we are serious about defending freedom, it is precisely in these times of conflict that we need to stand up for 'freedom for the thought that we hate' – and then exercise our right to take up intellectual arms against it. The solution is, as ever, more speech and argument rather than less. Even in an era of war and terror, it is a matter of life and death for liberty that we reject the fire-in-a-theatre device for tricking us out of our rights and insist on fighting the free-speech wars against all-comers. The demand that we sacrifice free speech in the name of freedom is a theatrical twist that deserves to be booed off the stage of history.

6

'Mind your Ps, Qs, Ns and Ys'

The prosecution alleges that some words are simply too evil to be tolerated, whatever the circumstances. We are faced with a lengthening and increasingly complicated list of words that cannot be spoken or written and can only be referred to by their first letter, stretching if not quite from a to z then at least from b to y.

As the official anti-racist campaign of the English Football Association made clear, after an American comedian caused a media outrage by referring to himself as a 'nigga' whilst performing at an FA awards ceremony, the British sports elite now 'condemns racial slurs, the use of the n-word, irrespective of context'. The words that should seriously grate with any thinking person here are 'irrespective of context'.

That statement might sound high-minded, but in truth it is imbecility of the lowest order. Of course context matters. How can the use of the term 'nigga' in a black comedian's routine, or by one black man to another, be deemed the same as if being shouted by a racist? As students living in the multi-ethnic tower blocks of Moss Side and Hulme, Manchester, during the long, hot summer of 1981, we watched Greater Manchester Police beating their riot batons on the side of their vans while chanting: 'Nigger, nigger, nigger – out, out, out!' They were not being ironic, and you did not need a degree in semantics to tell the difference.

According to the gospel of Zero Tolerance, as preached by public bodies in the Anglo-American world, there are words that it is now a mortal sin to utter, regardless of what was meant by them. This sounds like a modern form of mystical mumbo-jumbo, echoing the Old Testament law that anybody would be damned and probably stoned to death if they dared to speak the name of God (Yahweh, if you're interested in tweeting Him). Or perhaps like Harry Potter's chums, afraid to mention the name of Voldemort for fear that it might conjure up the dark lord before they get to the books' finale.

The concept of words being condemned 'regardless of context' has taken hold of the upper echelons of UK and US politics and culture as well as sport in recent years. Apparently it is now even possible to be guilty of a racial slur whilst trying to draw attention to racism. The Oscar-nominated British actor Benedict Cumberbatch sparked a 'race storm' in America by using the old-fashioned word 'coloured' while discussing the problem of racial inequality in the UK creative arts. Cumberbatch was obliged to issue a grovelling apology for having 'caused offence' by 'being an idiot', before praying that 'I can only hope this incident will highlight the need for correct usage of terminology that is accurate and inoffensive.'[1] But who is to say what terminology is inoffensive these days? The incident certainly highlighted the way that language has become a minefield even for those trying to fight on the side of the angels.

Something important has changed. It has become a war on words.

In the past, the free-speech wars tended to focus on ideas or arguments considered too subversive or dangerous to be allowed public expression. The recent backlash against public figures accused of speech crimes focuses not on ideas and opinions, but on words. These people have been dragged over the coals for using words that nobody is apparently allowed to use in any circumstances, whatever they meant by them, and regardless of whether they are spoken in public or private – or even inside somebody's own head.

The importance of context in judging words should have become more obvious in recent years, as people from minority groups have sought to 'reclaim' the sort of language previously used against them. Young black people took to calling one another nigger/nigga, some of the lesbian and gay community appropriated 'queer', and you might even hear the British-born children of Asian immigrants talking about themselves with pride as 'Pakis'. All of which should have made it more obvious than ever that context is what matters in judging words, and that it is madness to equate such banter (another hated b-word in some circles) with bigotry.

Yet things have gone in the other direction. The language police have grown even less tolerant of the 'wrong' words regardless of who uses them where, when or why.

Some might have hoped that the problem labelled 'Political Correctness gone mad' had passed its peak back in 1999, when David Howard, a white aide to the black Washington DC mayor Anthony A. Williams, was forced out of his post for describing a budget as 'niggardly' (an oldish adjective meaning 'mean', which has nothing to do with the similar-sounding racial insult). The public backlash against this ridiculous incident led Williams to reappoint Howard, though not in his original post. Julian Bond, the chairman of the NAACP (a venerable black civil rights organisation which has always, we might note, had the word 'Colored' in its name), spoke for many in complaining that: 'You hate to think you have to censor your language to meet other people's lack of understanding.' Bond added that 'the mayor has been niggardly in his judgment on the issue', and suggested the administration should buy dictionaries for all its staff members.[2]

Less than twenty years later, however, the demonisation of words seems less like an aberration than an accepted norm of Anglo-American society. It was always a mistake to attribute this problem to one of 'PC gone mad', since that pinned the blame on a few zealots and underestimated the wider influence and strengthening hold of these trends. Now we can see it is far more a case of the censorious standards of 'PC' gone mainstream, gaining widespread acceptance if not exactly enthusiastic support.

Things have reached the point where a single word that nobody is sure they heard on a TV tape that was never broadcast can be turned into a national issue of political controversy. Jeremy Clarkson, former outspoken presenter of the BBC's worldwide hit motoring show *Top Gear*, found himself caught in a media car crash after a newspaper got hold of some never-broadcast *Top Gear* footage. In the film, Clarkson is seen reciting the old playground rhyme 'Eeny, meeny, miny, moe …' to help him choose between two sports cars, and twice mumbles through the part where his (and my) generation of English schoolchildren might have said 'catch a nigger by his toe'. Some 'experts' claimed to be sure that he actually used the n-word; most people just heard a mumble.

A furore followed, with Clarkson first denying he had ever used that word and then, under orders from BBC bosses, issuing a grovelling video apology for offending anybody before completing another awkward U-turn and insisting that, while he often used the f-word and the c-word, he would never use the n-word.

Others, however, reacted as if he had been swinging a black baby around by the toe while hollering the racist rhyme at full volume on prime-time TV.

In all the overblown controversy over a murky snippet of never-seen video from the BBC archives, the most worrying words were not Clarkson's inaudible mumblings. They were the clear and unambiguous statement made by Harriet Harman MP, then deputy leader of the Labour Party and a minister in the previous government. In a post on Twitter (where else would a politician say Something Important these days?), Harman declared that: 'Anybody who uses the n-word in public or private in whatever context has no place in the British Broadcasting Corporation.'[3] The idea of politicians telling the public service broadcaster who to hire and fire would normally cause outrage in BBC circles, but not apparently where a rogue n-word is suspected of intruding.

For today's free-speech police, there is no difference between saying something in public or private or apparently saying it in your own head. Most importantly, they insist that somebody should be censored or sacked for being accused of using an offensive word 'in whatever context'.

This illiberal idiocy drives an SUV through the principles of liberty and justice. The specific context in which anybody uses language matters. We properly judge people not merely by the words they use, but by what they mean. By which standard, mumbling an outdated nursery rhyme – and then trying to ensure that nobody sees the film of your mumble – is in no way comparable to using the n-word as a racist epithet.

Yet common sense seems to play no part in our public life today. British law now decrees that if anybody at all interprets any word or deed as racist then it is a hate crime, regardless of the intention of the 'offender'. The c-word some seem keenest to see removed from the language is 'context'.

Once words themselves can be seen as evil regardless, the logical outcome is that wicked words of power have to be policed even in private speech.

Like the riot cops forcing back the picket lines of striking workers twenty-five years ago, the cultural thought police have been busy pushing back important lines in the free-speech wars. They have blurred the traditional distinction between what people say in public and in private.

The creeping intrusion into private words, the fudging of the lines between personal thoughts and public statements, has led to a string of controversies in the UK, US and Australia after the content of various public figures' phone calls, emails and text messages were made public. No doubt there will be many more such 'secret racism/sexism/homophobia' scandals to come, as more minds are turned inside out to see what is in there that shouldn't be. We need not endorse any of the unsavoury things that celebrities or sportsmen think or say in private in order to insist that they not be stuck in the public stocks for it.

Another sign of how far and fast things have changed. In 1999, when the senior UK judge Sir William Macpherson of Cluny published his official report into the murder of black London teenager Stephen Lawrence, almost all of its far-reaching proposals were accepted and written into law. The one proposal which even Tony Blair's New Labour balked at implementing, however, was Macpherson's suggestion that it should be a crime to use racist language in the privacy of your own home. Now that proposal is being practically implemented by stealth rather than statute.

This word-hunting invasion of privacy should be a concern to us all. Not because we want to defend the 'right' to be a racist at home, but because we recognise the importance of the private sphere. Everybody needs a space where they can rant, rave and gather their thoughts free from the public gaze. The right to a private sphere where we can consider what to say to the world is the vital flipside of the right to free speech in public life. As the writer André Aciman puts it, 'If we can't say what we think under our roof, then we have no roof.'[4]

The modern-day belief in 'words of power' appears to be underpinned by an equally firm belief that most of us are what we might call 'people of weakness'. The elitist assumption is that people are so stupid, vulnerable and pathetic that they can be mortally offended or murderously incited merely by hearing, or even thinking they hear, a naughty word.

In this context (excuse use of c-word) it becomes clear why the popular public arenas of sport and television have been made the front lines in the war on words. These are among the few outlets where our political and cultural elites still feel able to connect with the masses. So they want to use the power of TV and sport to teach us all a lesson in the need to mind our ps and qs and ns and ys.

The war on words trivialises issues such as racism and risks creating a wider chilling effect on freedom of expression, making people too worried about linguistic etiquette to say what they really think and too anxious about possibly causing offence to speak clearly. In effect, like Clarkson and his nursery rhyme, we all start mumbling over the controversial parts of the argument. That does nobody any favours. What we need is clarity and the open clash of opinions, not unintelligible mumbles, awkward silences and empty apologies.

This does not mean upholding a right to hurl racist language around (although it is better if bigots come clean with their prejudices so that they can be challenged in public). What it does mean, however, is fighting for freedom of expression with no buts, as an inalienable and indivisible liberty for all.

Those who want to police the words we use more firmly will insist, as the free-speech fraudsters always do in their silent war, that 'this is not a free-speech issue'. Instead it is about protecting the rights of others by refusing to endorse the use of racist or offensive language. But of course this is a free-speech issue. It is about the need for people to say what they think – rather than what they think they ought to say. That is our only chance of resolving arguments and tensions and getting closer to what we believe to be the truth.

Defending free speech these days can certainly mean standing up for some less than savoury characters, but to try to suppress words is simply to impose a polite etiquette, a snobs' speech code to make 'them' talk like 'us'. Imposing an etiquette or enforcing a speech code is not the same thing as having an argument, let alone winning one. It means telling people what they should say rather than engaging with what they think. In the interests of open debate and clarity of opinion, I have always felt that on balance people's prejudices are better out than in.

The alternative – of accusing people of racism for something they did not mean to say, and leaving others unwilling to speak because they are unsure of which words they should or shouldn't use – can only reinforce divisions and disaffection. That is quite a result for a policy which claims to be challenging prejudice and promoting tolerance. Meanwhile those who have been left behind by fast-changing fashions in acceptable language – see Gareth from the UK version of *The Office*, complaining that his old dad 'still says "darkies" instead of "coloureds"' – can find themselves denied a legitimate voice in public.

Those who think that banning words deemed offensive regardless of context is the way to change attitudes have it upside down. Words such as 'nigger' have faded from public use as more enlightened attitudes have taken hold across British and Western society. This is an important difference. The crusaders against evil words of power appear to believe that a volcano of hatred and violence lurks just beneath the surface of the Anglo-American world, only just held in check by their speech codes. Some of us believe that, on the contrary, if anything is likely to stir resentment amongst these largely tolerant peoples, it is constantly being ordered from above to watch their language.

The thin-skin syndrome that makes people hypersensitive to anything offensive rests upon the divisive mood of mistrust in our atomised society and the sense that everybody is potentially a victim of somebody else's words.

It would be better if we trusted others – and ourselves – to say what we really think and then respond accordingly. That might mean ignoring their nonsense, or telling them where to stick it – or having a proper argument where appropriate. What it should not mean, however, is calling in the language police. Instead we are entering a cultural age where people can be sacked, censured or censored for saying the wrong word, regardless of where they said it or what they meant by it. The inevitable consequence will be a freezing effect, making many people more cautious and further restricting conversation over a chilled glass of wine, never mind heated debate.

It even seems that the war on words does not only proscribe certain types of speech 'regardless of the context', and insist on what one academic has called the tyranny of 'sanitary euphemisms' such as the n-word. It also dictates that there can be no legitimate debate about this assault on freedom of expression, unless it adopts those same sanitary euphemisms and gets itself tied up in Trigger Warnings. Such are the dire consequences for free speech of accepting the medieval notion that 'words of power' are too dangerous for mental weaklings such as us to be trusted to handle alone.

7

'Free speech is just a licence for the mass media to brainwash the public'

The prosecution alleges that 'ordinary people' cannot cope with the power of the media and corporate advertising, so it needs to be restrained.

Arguments about regulating free speech now take place in a febrile atmosphere where the popular press and the mass media are depicted as society's supervillains. There is no real free speech for powerless 'ordinary' people, the prosecution alleges, who are at the mercy of the megaphone media. This is perhaps one of the most insidious arguments for reining in free speech: that, in the words of comedian, actor and anti-tabloid crusader Steve Coogan, 'press freedom is a lie',[1] because that freedom is only really available to the rich and powerful, via the mass media and the power of corporate advertising. The demand to restrict media freedom can then be presented as progressive, providing an apparently anti-capitalist excuse for censorship and control.

The blame-the-media mood has been used to justify the push for new regulations on publishing and broadcasting in the UK. There have been moves to tighten controls on what advertisers can say and where. And the British political class has united to try to impose the first system of state-backed press regulation in more than 300 years, via a Royal Charter. Even in the US, growing hostility in high places towards the tabloid press and Fox News along-side complaints about advertisers allegedly holding sway over consumers and voters has sparked calls for the First Amendment to be interpreted less leniently in regard to 'lower-value' types of speech, such as advertising.

None of this, we are assured, has anything to do with attacking freedom of speech. It is simply about curbing the ability of the mass media to spread lies and manipulate public opinion, whether in advertising or election campaigns. That might sound all well and good and might be thought attractive to an old Marxist like me. The trouble is there are two ugly illiberal prejudices underpinning the liberal media-bashing.

It involves a low view of the importance of the freedom of the press. That liberty has been fought for and defended over five centuries as the practical expression of free speech, by people who were prepared to suffer and even to die for their cause. If only these heroes could have had access to the wisdom of Steve Coogan/Alan Partridge, they could have saved themselves a lot of trouble. After all, what fool would go to the Tower of London or the gallows in support of 'a lie'? The entire discussion of press regulation in the UK today is premised on the myth that the press is somehow 'too free' to run wild and make trouble. It would be far more true to say that the press is not nearly free or open enough.

The blame-the-media mood is also based on a low view of the public. Attacks on the influence of the mass media are often coded assaults on the intelligence of the masses. The assumption is that people are so gullible and greedy they can easily be manipulated by the media into doing the 'wrong' thing, whether at the supermarket check-out or the ballot box.

The cry 'I blame the meejah!' has become a constant feature of Western cultural debates. There is scarcely a social problem from global warming to Islamophobia that is not casually attributed to the malign influence of the allegedly unethical mass media – often by those looking down from the allegedly ethical upper echelons of the liberal media.

What do campaigns to ban fast food advertisements, or to make tobacco companies sell cigarettes only in plain packages, or in various other ways to counter and control media influence and bias, have to do with freedom of expression? More than some would have us believe.

These things *are* free-speech issues. Not only because they infringe on the right of corporations and newspapers to say what they want (if free speech is supposed to be for all, then why not for Philip Morris and Ronald McDonald, too, just as it should be for their critics?). But also, more importantly, because it infringes on the other side of free speech – the right of the public to hear and see whatever we want, judge for ourselves, and make our own choices.

The progressive-sounding attack on media influence is almost always underpinned by reactionary notions about the masses who are deemed too pathetic or childlike to cope with or resist whatever the mass media tells them. So people must be 'protected' from dangerous ideas and images, inconvenient facts, and ultimately from themselves.

Most attacks on the power of the mass media, corporate PR and advertisers' puff in Anglo-American culture are really a coded way of dumping on the supposedly feeble-minded public. The ostensible targets are such powerful hate-figures as media moguls and corporate fat-cats. The underlying target, however, is the mass of 'sheeple' who supposedly do the bidding of these super-rich Svengalis. To accuse the media of 'dumbing down' is really to say that they are pandering to the base tastes of the mass of dummies.

In a free society of morally autonomous adults, the right to make your own choices – even the right to make the 'wrong' choices – should be resolutely defended in the consumer marketplace as well as the 'marketplace of ideas' covering politics or religion.

As with so many battles in the free-speech wars today, the underlying lack of faith in free speech reflects and reinforces a lack of belief in humanity. It says we cannot be trusted to resist the siren calls of the media and the advertisers. Which raises the question – who is really showing contempt for the public as mugs and muppets in this discussion?

Of course the media can exert a powerful influence in shaping perceptions of events. But to go further and try to blame the media for what happens in the real world makes little sense. The clue is in the name: media. Whether we are talking about traditional print newspapers or up-to-the-microsecond online outlets, they are still only a collective 'medium' for transmitting information and images between people. The media reflects real life and helps to shape perceptions of it. But it cannot create reality at will. As Karl Marx wrote in one of his first German newspaper columns back in the 1840s, the press is ultimately about as responsible for changes in the world on which it reports 'as the astronomer's telescope is for the unceasing motion of the universe. Evil astronomy!'[2]

The only way in which the blame-the-media case makes sense is if one accepts the fairy tale assumption that the public really does what it is told by the media mirror on the wall.

Complaints about manipulative media advertising often contain similar 'hidden messages' about brainless consumers. Campaigners might be keen to stress that they are gunning for the corporate giants of Big Tobacco, Big Alcohol or Big Food. Yet the ultimate target in their sights is the Big Public, viewed as only one jingly advert for fast food or cheap booze away from being reduced to a blob of obese alcoholics. The anti-advertising crusaders always urge us to 'think of the children!', but their campaigns treat consumers as incapable infants.

* * *

Listening to those who want more controls on the hated 'popular press' and the 'mass media', one might almost think it was better to be unpopular. It helps, I have long thought, to recall that the word 'popular' has its origins in the Latin *populus* – the people. Attacks on the 'popular press' and 'mass media' are often code words for the elite's fear and loathing of the populace, the masses who are supposedly stupid enough to be duped by media messages telling them how to vote (in reality TV shows and real elections), who to hate, and which celebrities to worship.

In our allegedly enlightened age, it is no longer considered decent (at least outside the more old-fashioned gentlemen's clubs) to talk about 'ordinary people' as if they were proletarian scum or 'fucking plebs' or tasteless chewing gum stuck to the bottom of one's riding boot.

If you cannot insult the populace directly, however, you can do it via attacks on the popular press that imply the moral inferiority of those who put the mass in the mass media. This is the respectable way to draw a line between the enlightened few and the herd who are prey to the dark arts of the media manipulators.

There is a long history here. Arguments about controlling the media's output have often been underwritten by attitudes to controlling the people's thoughts. Those who fear and loathe the mass of people and their passions tend to favour more control over what they are allowed to see, hear or read. Those who believe in an unfettered media are more likely to believe in people's capacity to consider everything and choose what is right for themselves.

When popular movements to change society are on the up, support for media freedom tends to rise with them – from the flourishing printing presses in England and America during their respective revolutionary eras of the seventeenth and eighteenth centuries, to the many political online blogs that sprang up during more recent popular protests around the world. But when faith in humanity is out of fashion, as across much of Western culture today, media-bashing comes more into vogue as a proxy for expressing contempt for the masses who have disappointed their betters.

The struggle over how free the media should be to educate, inform, entertain, outrage and entice the populace has raged for more than 500 years, since William Caxton introduced the first printing press into England in 1476.

However, it is in the modern age that the practice of attacking the mass media as a proxy for attacking the masses has really come into its own.

No longer able to give the lower orders a public flogging, the elites instead appointed the popular press as a whipping boy. Flaying the vulgarity of the new mass media became a proxy for beating the vulgar masses.

In the late-nineteenth and early-twentieth centuries the new proxy war on the mass media was often led by high-minded intellectuals and literati who, lacking the political skills of those who wanted the masses' votes, failed to conceal that their loathing of the press was really aimed at the readers. For German philosopher Friedrich Nietzsche, the rabble 'vomit their bile, and call it a newspaper'.[3] English author D. H. Lawrence wanted schools closed and reading discouraged to protect workers from those 'tissues of leprosy', popular books and newspapers.[4] The writer H. G. Wells hated newspapers because he considered their readers as fearsomely alien as the Martians in his novel *The War of the Worlds*. Professor John Carey, author of *The Intellectuals and the Masses*, is clear on the prejudice underpinning Wells's hatred of 'popular newspapers': 'Newspapers were dangerous, Wells believed, because the profit motive forced them to appeal to the most crude and vulgar passions, such as patriotism and war-fever. This made them prime organs of mass hatred. A popular newspaper was, in a quite literal sense, a "poison rag"'.[5]

The elites of the first half of the twentieth century decried the mass media as a cipher for expressing their disgust at the masses.

Their real concern was not so much low media standards as the low culture of the lower classes who consumed it.

In more recent times, the elites' proxy war against the mass media in the UK and US – now including television and the internet as well as traditional newspapers – has been joined by the modern left, seeking scapegoats for their frequent failure to win over the mass of voters.

Hume's law of inverse proportion states that 'the less fulsome support Labour and the Left receive from voters, the more fierce their attacks on the mass media become; the less certain they are of the loyalty of working people, the more certain they become that the popular press is exerting malign influence'.[6] All political parties on both sides of the Atlantic have at times been guilty of peddling this it-was-the-media-wot-lost-it excuse, though Labour and the US Democrats have pushed it hardest of late. The Anglo-American left has projected its disappointment with the masses onto the mass media.

In the eighteenth century, English MPs wanted to restrict the reporting of parliament in order to prevent the people being 'misled by printers', and to protect them from newspapers 'for their good'. Today's politicians similarly seem to believe that gullible and apathetic voters are at the mercy of the modern mass media and should be protected for their own good.

It is undeniable that newspapers, television and now the web have a big influence in politics. It is also evident that, with the decline of political party membership and activism, the media sphere has become the big battleground in UK and US politics, with more and more political events fitting Daniel Boorstin's definition of a 'pseudo-event' – non-spontaneous events that are staged primarily in order to be reported in the media.[7] Understanding that process, however, is a long way from swallowing the notion that the mass media has exerted an authoritarian malign influence over politics. That remains an easy excuse with which politicians of all parties can seek to explain away their own loss of influence and authority among the public. The underlying sentiment expressed is too often a disdain for the masses, and a wish to regulate people's thoughts and actions by curbing the media that supposedly manipulates them like puppets.

When all of that is said and done, and we have separated the propaganda from the proof, it remains indisputable that the rich and powerful inevitably have more opportunity than others to exercise their right to free speech via the media. Even in Anglo-American societies where formal free speech prevails, having a voice that can be heard is not something most of us can take for granted.

The question is, what is to be done about it? And the answer should be that whatever response we choose, supporting efforts to get the state to curb the freedom of the media can only make matters worse. The only way any of us can have a proper opportunity to exercise freedom of speech is if that right is defended across society and not undermined further for anybody.

Free speech is an indivisible liberty. You cannot start tampering with it for one group – even if the group is press barons or PR executives – and expect it to remain intact for everybody else. Once the bulwark has been breached and the cultural support for the principle of freedom of the press and of speech is compromised, everything is called into question. And once free speech is openly called into question it ceases to be a right.

Free speech is not a zero-sum game, where you somehow have to decrease the rights of others in order to increase your own. It is not a negotiable commodity that can somehow be 'redistributed' away from the rich and powerful towards the rest. To infringe on the right to free speech of others can only risk undermining your own capacity to exercise it.

A key issue in the modern debate is our attitude to the state. State regulation and control has long been the enemy of freedom of speech and of the press. Granting the authorities more power to decide who deserves those freedoms, however progressive-sounding the pretext might be, can only open the door for the state to extend its deadening influence over public debate.

There is always a difference between formal legal equal rights and real inequalities in society. As the old saw goes, it is equally illegal for either the rich or the poor to sleep on park benches, but somehow only the poor get arrested for it. Similarly, since the abolition of state licensing it has been equally possible for anybody to establish a national newspaper or (if they can get the regulators' permission) a television station. Yet somehow only the very rich seem to do so.

The power which a few large entities can exercise over much of the Anglo-American media is a longstanding problem. It is likely to remain so at least until we are all billionaires or the billionaires all become socialists. In the meantime, we can moan about media empires and encourage the state to restrict their freedoms. Or we can strive to remove all legal and cultural obstacles to freedom of expression, in order to maximise the opportunities for broadening the debate and creating an alternative media.

One historical trend that the discussion of Western media empires tends to avoid is the consistent failure to create any popular alternative media. There have always been big barriers to successful media 'start-ups', yet the internet has already given a glimpse of opportunities to create a new media on an unprecedented scale. The problem is that, for all of its flashy formats, far too much of the 'new' media has adapted to the wider climate of dull conformism in its content. If all those who spend their time and energy bemoaning the 'toxic' influence of the mass media instead devoted their efforts to creating a serious alternative via the web, and developing some new ideas to spread through it, who knows where we might end up?

One area which we should definitely be concerned about is the ability of the rich and powerful to prevent critical voices being heard, through the libel laws. Despite recent liberalising reforms, the UK's notoriously censorious laws of defamation remain among the worst in the civilised world (as I believed and argued even before I lost a punitive libel case in 2000). The huge costs and penalties involved, and the way the rules are stacked against defendants, do not only punish those relative few who fight and lose a libel suit in London's Royal Courts of Justice. They also have a far wider 'chilling effect' on the exercise of free speech, making many reluctant to risk the wrath of the corporate lawyers by publishing anything too critical. The American system which, since 1964, has effectively made it impossible for a public figure to sue for libel, unless the publication was motivated by malice, is far friendlier to free speech and open debate of important issues. The US also now refuses to enforce judgements obtained by 'libel tourists' in London courts. Defenders of press freedom might do even better to revive and update the spirit of the great London newspaper essayist of the eighteenth century, 'Cato', who declared: 'I must own, that I would rather many libels should escape than the liberty of the press should be infringed.'[8]

It would be good to strive for a freer, more open and open-minded media via the web, that could provide outlets for more voices and different opinions. But it would not be good to imagine that situation can be brought about by greater state intervention and regulation of press freedom.

As ever, the question is: who do you trust to regulate public debate and decide what should be published, and by whom? Some of us would always rather leave it up to the public rather than the state to see everything and judge for themselves what is good for the 'public interest'.

In various ways, the arguments for greater restrictions on the power of the mass media all rest on the myth that the press and the media are too free to do as they like. This turns an important truth on its head. Especially in the UK, the media is nowhere near free or open enough even before any new rules and regulations are imposed.

There are already far too many formal rules and regulations, such as the execrable libel laws, impinging on freedom of the press. More dangerous still is the informal culture of conformism across much of the media that makes official censorship largely unnecessary. In his 1945 essay, 'The Freedom of the Press', George Orwell admitted that, for much of the Second World War, state censorship in Britain had not been 'particularly irksome'. Instead the media and cultural elites had generally censored themselves, particularly by rejecting criticism of Britain's ally, Stalin's Soviet Union: 'Unpopular ideas can be silenced, and inconvenient facts kept dark, without the need for any official ban ... [T]hings which on their own merits would get the big headlines [have been] kept right out of the British press, not because the Government intervened but because of a general tacit agreement that it "wouldn't do" to mention that particular fact.'[9] This 'tacit agreement' to suppress the truth not only covered the newspapers owned by rich press barons, but 'the same kind of veiled censorship also operates in books and periodicals, as well as in plays, films and radio. At any given moment there is an orthodoxy, a body of ideas which it is assumed that all right-thinking people will accept without question ... Anyone who challenges the prevailing orthodoxy finds himself silenced with surprising effectiveness. A genuinely unfashionable opinion is almost never given a fair hearing, either in the popular press or in the highbrow periodicals.'

Today's pervasive culture of You-Can't-Say-That has much the same effect on narrowing the minds of the media as the 'It wouldn't do' wartime consensus – and a new generation of the 'renegade liberals' whom Orwell identified as deserting the cause of freedom are enforcing the orthodoxy. We are often warned in the multi-media age that people are bombarded with too many adverts and images. A bigger problem in the one-note media age is that we are presented with far too few choices in the marketplace of ideas and news reports.

No doubt there are many problems with the press and the wider media. But history suggests there is always one thing worse than a free press, and that is its opposite. Nowhere in the world today is the problem with the media that it is 'too free'.

Putting up with the broadcast of what you might not like in the media and letting others choose what they see or read or consume or vote for is part of the price of defending freedom of expression for us all. As the young Karl Marx told the Prussian state censors more than 170 years ago, when they tried to suggest that only what they deemed a moral and decent press should be free: 'You cannot enjoy the advantages of a free press without putting up with its inconveniences. You cannot pluck the rose without its thorns! And what do you lose with a free press?'[10] Without defending freedom for the press and the media against state intrusion and sanitisation, however, we risk losing a big battle in the free-speech wars.

8

'Liars and Holocaust deniers do not deserve to be heard'

The prosecution alleges that censorship is sometimes necessary because there can be no right to spread lies or subvert incontrovertible truths – whether about the history of the Nazi Holocaust, the science of climate change, or much else.

Once upon a time we had political, historical and scientific debates. Those with alternative views were seen as intellectual opponents to be argued with and defeated. Today anybody questioning the dominant views on emotive subjects risks being accused of 'denial'. And those branded as 'deniers', accused of deliberately corrupting incontrovertible truths, have to be shut up or even locked up, not debated with.

The allegation of 'denial' has become a powerful device to demand that a discussion be closed down and an argument silenced. It began with the allegation of Holocaust denial, used to demonise and criminalise those few cranks and neo-fascists in the West who would question the truth of the Nazi genocide against the Jews. Now the allegation of denial is promiscuously deployed on all sorts of issues. Those whose views fall outside the mainstream of orthodox opinion have been variously accused of genocide denial, climate-change denial, Aids denial, racism denial, rape denial, inequality denial and even 'denial denial'.

The ease with which the denial label can be applied to dissidents on one issue after another suggests that it has little to do with the specific debates on these questions. Crusaders now yell 'Denier!' just as their predecessors yelled 'Witch!' – as a spell to discredit any opponent and short-circuit any argument. The vehemence of these accusations signifies less their strength of feeling on a particular issue than their general antagonism towards the free-for-all of open discussion.

Those waging war on denial will insist that this has 'nothing to do with free speech'. They are simply trying to protect the truth from liars, and in the process to protect the victims from harm.

But denial is a free-speech issue. Indeed, opposing bans on those who would deny the Holocaust is an acid test for supporting free speech with no 'buts'. It is a stand-out case for defending the principle of 'freedom for the thought that we hate'. Challenging the wider use of the denial card to close down other debates is also becoming of undeniable importance, if we want to live in an open-minded society.

To call somebody a 'denier' is to allege that they have crossed a moral line. Their views are not just wrong, but have no right to be heard. That's why accusations of denial are among the favourite weapons *du jour* of the reverse-Voltaires, who do not wish to debate their opponents' views but to deny their right to express them. In this, the allegation of 'denial' has become the respectable face of intellectual intolerance today. That stands it in a long and inglorious historical tradition.

Like free speech, tolerance is a fairly modern idea. For centuries, Church and state in European societies combined to persecute those heretics who dared to deny some aspect of the orthodox beliefs of the age. Intolerance was the order of the day and free-thinking was an abomination to those who lived by religious orthodoxy.

Most infamously, the sixteenth-century friar–philosopher–astrologer Giordano Bruno, branded a heretic by the Pope and the

Inquisition, was burned at the stake in Rome's Campo de Fiori in February 1600, with his tongue tied down to suppress his 'wicked words', and all his books were banned.

What all of these heretics had in common was that, in putting forward new opinions and challenging the old, they were questioning the unquestionable. Their arguments inevitably involved the denial of important aspects of the dominant religious orthodoxy. As one account has it, 'heretics were seen as religiously subversive, socially dangerous and even morally debased'.[1] Little wonder that some were sufficiently fearful of being branded a heretic that they hid their denial of the Church's teachings. Nicolaus Copernicus, the Polish astronomer whose belief that the Earth was not the centre of the Universe inspired Galileo and others, made sure that his book was not published until after his death in 1543.

The world, of course, has moved on a lot since those dark days, and not only in the sense that Copernicus meant. No Church exercises anything like unquestioned authority in the secular Western societies of the twenty-first century. Without a dominant orthodoxy, there can surely be no heretics condemned and punished in the West for denying the core truths of the age.

And yet … In the absence of an unquestioned moral code supposedly handed down by God, the moral guardians of the modern age have had to find new ways to draw a line between Good and Evil (or as they might be more likely to call it today, between Appropriate and Inappropriate words or behaviours). They have seized upon rare examples of unambiguous wickedness – child sexual abuse, say, or slavery – as secular evils against which all decent men and women must unite. These become the new taboos and none are allowed to question the orthodox teaching on such issues. The greatest new taboo of all is questioning the facts of the Nazis' genocidal massacre of six million Jews – what is now known as Holocaust denial.

Those who question the history of the Holocaust are treated as the secular equivalent of heretics today, pariahs to be cast out of civilised society and, in many European countries, cast into jail. It might seem a bit much to compare these fools, frauds and fanatics to the heroic heretics of the past, but it is worth recalling that the term heresy derives from the ancient Greek for 'to choose', in particular to choose to dissent from the dominant orthodoxy of the day. As Arthur Versluis observes in *The New Inquisitions*, 'A "heretic", then, is one who chooses, one who therefore exemplifies freedom of individual thought.' Thus what the Inquisition and the heretic-hunters of the twenty-first century do indeed have in common is that 'the "crime" in question is fundamentally a "crime" of thought'.[2] The fact that hate-mongering Holocaust deniers don't deserve to be mentioned in the same breath as Galileo or Spinoza cannot alter the fact that they too are being pursued for thought crimes.

In many ways the Holocaust has become less an historic atrocity to be taught, discussed and understood in its political context and more a matter of religious orthodoxy, a moral parable about human evil to be learnt by rote. This puts the accepted version of what happened and why beyond question, something that secular authorities were no more prepared to have debated than the Pope might be willing to haggle over the truth of transubstantiation. The notion of banning (either explicitly or implicitly) those who dissent from this truth, the Holocaust deniers, followed logically from its elevation into pseudo-theology.

In recent decades the Holocaust has been turned into a moral absolute everywhere from classroom to courtroom. Once that was done, the next step was to convert it into an all-purpose brand that could be adapted to suit any agenda or campaign. Want to get a leg up onto the moral high ground in any debate? Just conjure up some comparison with the Holocaust, however far-fetched. So it is that pro-life crusaders will talk about the 'Abortion Holocaust', and that the US animal rights crusaders at PETA could seriously launch a campaign damning farmed meat as the 'Holocaust on your plate'.

From the 1990s, those campaigning for Western military intervention around the world, for example in the conflicts in the former Yugoslavia, were also quick to compare these civil wars to the Nazi Holocaust.

Just as Holocaust denial has been made a taboo and a crime, so those accused of the secular blasphemy of denial on other issues now faced demands that they be silenced and censored.

Crusaders against the new variants of denial don't only wish to silence their opponents. In the true tradition of heresy-hunting, they also want to inflict punishment on those who deny the true faith. There are even demands for those condemned as climate-change deniers to face Nuremberg-style trials for 'crimes against humanity and nature.'

How did 'denial' achieve this status of something akin to secular blasphemy? A traditional dictionary definition would say that denial involves asserting something 'to be untrue or untenable'. That is what the unorthodox thinkers of the past were doing – denying the truth of an accepted opinion of their age, and offering an alternative interpretation.

But the allegation of 'denial' today is used to mean something different. It relates to a more modern definition, which states that denial can also mean a 'refusal to acknowledge an unacceptable truth or emotion, or to admit it into consciousness'. In our therapy-soaked psychobabbling culture, the definition that holds sway is this one relating to mental health; denial now allegedly involves a defensive suppression of knowledge that is too painful or traumatic to cope with. In short, deniers are pathological liars.

To accuse somebody of 'denial' no longer means merely that they are questioning or criticising some conventional wisdom. It implies instead that they are refusing to acknowledge what everybody knows is the undoubted truth – as with Holocaust denial. The crusaders who cry 'Denier!' are not just accusing their opponents of disagreeing, but of dishonestly refusing to face the undisputed facts. Those who are 'in denial' are thus low liars or sufferers from some mental aberration, who are not worth listening to and can safely be silenced if not straitjacketed.

There is nothing good to be said in defence of those who wish to deny the truth of the Holocaust, and attempt to write death camps and gas ovens out of our history. If there is one thing more stupid than that, however, it is surely imposing bans designed to turn Holocaust denial into a thought crime.

Some of us who entirely accept the historical truths of the Nazi Holocaust and the deaths of six million Jews nevertheless oppose bans and laws against Holocaust denial on two key grounds, one principled and one more practical. First, because we believe in freedom of speech as a fundamental political principle that has virtue in and of itself, regardless of the content of what might be said. And second because, in practice, trying to deal with a political issue such as Holocaust denial through bans can only make the problem worse, by encouraging cynicism and giving credence to conspiracy theories.

Whether some like it or not, treating Holocaust denial as a crime *is* a straightforward free-speech issue. It is a measure of how far the historic principle of freedom of speech has fallen out of fashion that so many should now believe that the way to deal with obnoxious opinion is through the law rather than argument.

Freedom of speech is the eau de vie of a civilised society, without which many other liberties that we care about would not be possible. It is also an indivisible freedom. To have any real meaning, free speech must also extend to those that the mainstream deems irresponsible or unpalatable – be that the noble Greek philosopher Socrates, the brilliant Italian astronomer Galileo, or the anti-Semitic French 'funny man' Dieudonné.

Opposing the criminalisation of Holocaust denial is more than the right thing to do. It is an acid test for those who believe in the principle of free speech. After all, extreme ideas are the ones that most often need defending against bans. That should not imply any sort of support or sympathy for the historical falsehoods of the Holocaust deniers. It is instead in the spirit of the indivisible principle of free speech.

Once that principle becomes negotiable, there is no telling where it will end. Trying to make a 'special case' of Holocaust denial will not work. History demonstrates that, every time curbs are introduced on one type of speech, they serve as a cue for demands to censor something else. It is no surprise that the criminalisation of Holocaust denial has led to demands to repress other 'deniers' who diverge from conventional wisdom.

So much for the principle. The practical arguments against bans on Holocaust deniers are just as important today. The best way to confront bad ideas and distortions is always through debate and exposure – through more speech rather than less. To seek to repress them instead can only inhibit the search for clarity and truth. Attempting a bureaucratic solution to profound political and social problems through bans and proscriptions always makes matters worse.

Nobody has been more forthright in challenging Holocaust denial than the American historian Deborah Lipstadt, Professor of Modern Jewish and Holocaust Studies and author of *Denying the Holocaust*. That book led to Lipstadt being unsuccessfully sued for libel by the British 'revisionist' historian David Irving, a case which cost her six years and a small fortune to contest before a London court finally found in her favour and declared Irving to be a racist and a Holocaust denier in 2000.

Yet when an Austrian court later jailed Irving for three years for the crime of Holocaust denial, Lipstadt warned against the dangers of trying to gag deniers. The way to defeat them was as she had done, through open public debate and exposure and establishing the facts, rather than with laws and bans. 'Ironically,' she said of her public demolition of Irving's historical distortions, 'none of this would have happened had the UK had laws outlawing Holocaust denial. I shudder at the thought that politicians might be given the power to legislate history. They can hardly fix the potholes in our streets. How can we expect them to decide what is the proper version of history?'[3]

After her libel trial win, Lipstadt also made clear that, whilst Holocaust denial was a lie, it should not be illegitimate to question the known details of the Nazis' historic crime – after all, she said, 'this is not theology'. That must be news to the many zealous crusaders who seek to restrict free speech by treating denial as the new form of secular blasphemy.

Promiscuous allegations of 'denial' and the blood sport of heretic-hunting have now spread from the Holocaust to other important issues. The fact that even some leading scientists are seemingly prepared to treat their critics as 'deniers' to be silenced, rather than sceptics to be answered, confirms the dangers of this newly respectable form of intolerance.

Take the issue of climate change. We are often assured these days that the science of man-made climate change is settled, the debate is finished, the question is closed. No further indulgence of 'climate-change deniers' is therefore necessary or acceptable.

Now, I claim no insight into the science of climatology, but you need not be a scientist to grasp the important role that open-ended debate and the encouragement of scepticism has played in the advance of science through history. And you need only be a democrat to insist that it is not up to scientists to dictate what can and cannot legitimately be discussed in a free society.

Think about this. If the censorious attitudes of these scientists and politicians had prevailed over the past centuries, it seems unlikely that a scientific outlook would ever have broken through in Western societies. It was only by overcoming the intolerance of the past, such as that which the Inquisition showed to Bruno and Galileo, that science was able to advance and flourish in the more tolerant age of Enlightenment. Do scientists seriously wish for a new attitude of intolerance to banish ideas with which they disagree, to burn the books if not the authors?

How then should we deal with those who question accepted wisdom and try to separate the truth from the lies? It's not a new problem. Almost 200 years ago John Stuart Mill complained about a 'flowering of quackery and ephemeral literature' and promotion of mock science through the new 'arts' of the media. Yet Mill argued for the tolerance of all ideas, even those we believe to be lies, as the best way to establish the truth for all to see.

For Mill, alongside his firm adherence to the principle of free speech, the practical virtue of allowing heretics and the holders of 'false opinion' to question received wisdom is that it forces the mainstream to defend and prove its viewpoint. He summed up beautifully two different bases for assuming your argument is true – a good one, based on tolerance and refutation of criticism, and a bad one based on intolerance of any scepticism or questioning: 'There is the greatest difference,' wrote Mill in *On Liberty*, 'between presuming an opinion to be true, because, with every opportunity for contesting it, it has not been refuted, and assuming its truth for the purpose of not permitting its refutation.'[4]

It was in this spirit that, back in the 1660s, the Royal Society was founded in London with the motto *Nullius in verba*, which translates as 'On the word of no one', or as we might say today 'Take nobody's word for it'. Everything was open to question and demands for proof, nothing was set in stone (except that motto), scepticism was the very stuff of scientific inquiry. By contrast today's champions of what one leading authority advocated as 'gross intolerance' in science seem to live not just in a different century from the founders of the Royal Society or the likes of Mill, but on another planet.[5] Their attitude is to treat those who disagree with them as lying deniers, to be dealt with by moral condemnation and censorship rather than argument and evidence.

The responsibility not only of scientists, but also of historians and journalists, remains to question everything. The new intolerance that would condemn its opponents as 'deniers' to be outlawed rather than exposed is undeniably a fashionably dangerous and dangerously fashionable excuse for attacking free speech, and denying the public the chance to judge the truth for themselves.

The fear of free speech

We have a lot to lose by giving up the fight for freedom of expression. The one thing we do need to lose instead is the fear of free speech.

Fear of free speech is about far more than the unlikely prospect of being shot for your opinions or cartoons. That is the far end of a spectrum of fear that begins with the embarrassment of saying something different from what is expected, and the sense that one should apologise the moment anybody takes exception.

That fear is not entirely unfounded. Free speech is far from being the risk-free easy option. Words can hurt, talk can start trouble and even wars, there are words and opinions that some might reasonably think would be better unsaid, and freedom does inevitably mean that other people are free to talk and tweet out of their backsides as well as their frontal lobes.

Yet whatever discomforting symptoms it might bring on or risks it might entail, in the end free speech is always a price worth paying, and the alternative of restricting it out of fear is always worse. Freedom of speech is not the problem. Fear of it is.

No doubt the right to free speech has been used to pursue all manner of offensive ends down the centuries. But we should not accept that as an excuse for limiting it today. The value of free speech outweighs the possible harm, and defending 'freedom for the thought that we hate' is the only sure way to protect it for all. As the Polish-born leader of German revolutionaries Rosa Luxemburg nailed it a century ago: 'Freedom is always and exclusively *freedom* for the one who thinks differently.'[1] Some of those who fought the historic battles for freedom of speech and of the press used it for low purposes, from John Wilkes, the English scandalmonger and pornographer in the eighteenth century, to Larry Flynt, the *Hustler* publisher in the twentieth, who pithily captured the essence of why it is important to defend the right to be offensive: 'If the First Amendment will protect a scumbag like me, it will protect all of you.'[2]

Defending the right to be offensive need not mean celebrating obnoxiousness. It is about upholding the freedom to think what you like and say what you think. Our sole responsibility should be to ensure that we have expressed the truth as we understand it, clarified the argument or cracked the joke to the best of our abilities, then allow others the same freedom to respond.

The fear of free speech for all is often ultimately based on fear and loathing of the masses, who might dare to use that freedom as they see fit rather than as they are told. Support for freedom of expression always blooms at moments in history when humanity is marching forward and filled with confidence in itself; it shrivels in more fearful and misanthropic times. That is why supporting unfettered free speech today is a declaration of faith in the future, an invitation to an open, no-holds-barred debate about the sort of societies in which we, and our children, might want to live. To accept instead that it should be restricted would be an admission that we fear the future too much to trust people to think and decide for themselves. We need more free speech and open debate if we are to stand a chance of resolving the conflicts in our society today and creating a less fearful tomorrow.

Over the past century, many of the great debates about free speech and its limits in the Anglo-American world have focused on cases heard in the US Supreme Court. Perhaps then we might leave the final thought on the fear of free speech to Justice Louis Brandeis, from a 1927 Supreme Court case that considered the conviction in California of Anna Whitney, a member of the Communist Labor Party of America, for engaging in speech deemed to have threatened society. Justice Brandeis insisted that, before speech could be restrained, 'there must be reasonable ground to fear that serious evil will result if free speech is practiced' and reasonable ground to believe that the danger is 'imminent'. He dismissed the notion that mere fear of what might happen could be ground for suppressing speech, in words that echo down the decades: 'Fear of serious injury cannot alone justify suppression of free speech and assembly. Men feared witches and burnt women. It is the function of speech to free men from the bondage of irrational fears.'[3]

Despite that rousing declaration, Brandeis then went on to vote with the rest of the Supreme Court judges to uphold Whitney's conviction for speech crimes. Proof, if any more were needed post-*Charlie Hebdo*, that whatever fine words we hear from the Western authorities, free speech is never a liberty that can be taken for granted.

The Trigger Warnings we need

Trigger Warnings have become symbols of the culture of You-Can't-Say-That. They appear at the start of books, films, articles or news reports to warn that the following contains words or images which some might find harmful or disturbing, followed by a list of all the things we are supposed to be wary of – from A for Ableism or B for Bi-phobia, to X for Xenophobia or Z for Zionism.

Trigger Warnings have become the modern equivalent of those 'Here Be Dragons' notices that used to be inscribed on uncharted areas of ancient maps. They are an invitation to self-censorship, to cover your eyes and ears pre-emptively – and in the process, to close your mind. And they point the way towards more official censorship by our increasingly offence-sensitive authorities. Trigger Warnings are the enemies of freedom of expression and open discussion.

We are living in the age of the reverse-Voltaires, who would far rather close down debate than suffer others' freedom of speech, and whose core belief can be summarised as 'I know I will detest what you say, and I will fight to the end of free speech for my right to prevent you saying it.' The reverse-Voltaires love Trigger Warnings, which enable them to tell us what we should – and more importantly, should not – see, read or hear, for our own good, of course.

Time we turned the situation around, and set up some alternative Trigger Warnings to alert us to attacks on free speech.

The phrases listed here are all invitations, if not orders, to shut up and withdraw from the rhetorical fray. The code words used are changing and mutating all the time, but the essential message is always the same: either You-Can't-Say-THAT, or YOU-Can't-Say-That – and quite possibly, both. The reaction of those who care about freedom should be to do the opposite, and insist on the right to think what we like and say what we think.

Here are just some of the coded arguments that should trigger a fighting response for free speech.

'This is not a free-speech issue.'
This a pretty sure sign that, yes, it is.

The first shot fired in the silent war on free speech is often an assurance that the bans or proscriptions on speech being demanded really have nothing to do with attacking freedom of expression. Of course the fraudsters assure us that they all support free speech, but this is about something else – hate or harassment, national security or personal safety.

What they usually mean is 'This is not a me-speech issue'. It is not infringing on their free speech, so it's not a problem. But free speech is not the same as me-speech, never mind me-me-me speech. It is always primarily about defending freedom for the other fellow, for the one who thinks differently. Not everything is a free-speech issue – direct threats of violence don't count, for instance, and neither does swearing too loudly in a bar or the library. But anything that interferes with anybody's right to express an opinion, tell a joke, chant a song – or their right to criticise somebody else for doing so – *is* a free-speech issue, whether some might like to think so or not. The biggest free-speech issue of all should be any attempt to restrict it whilst claiming that you're not.

'Of course I believe in free speech, but ...'

This is the one most often guaranteed to give the game away that no, in fact, you don't.

Ours is the age of the but-heads, when almost nobody opposes free speech 'in principle', but Principle is seemingly another country and they do things differently there. In Practice, back here on Earth, many have a 'but' to wave around in the face of free speech to explain why the freedom to express an opinion should go thus far, but no further, like 'free'-range livestock caged in a pen.

This might sound reasonable. But (to use the only language some people seem to understand) the problem is that, like all meaningful liberties, free speech has to be a universal and indivisible right. Once you apply a 'but', impose a condition or attach a string, it ceases to be a right. Instead it becomes a concession to be rationed by somebody in authority.

Those ubiquitous 'buts' don't just qualify a commitment to free speech, they crush it. To claim to believe in free speech, but ... is akin to insisting that you believe in an Almighty God, but you don't think He's all that. It might be better if the but-heads came clean and confessed that they don't really believe in free speech after all.

'We should defend free speech, but not hate speech.'

That might sound a no-brainer. After all, who could be in favour of hate speech? But the tougher questions are these: Which words exactly should qualify as hate speech? And who would you trust to decide which forms of speech should be sent to the chopping block?

There is no more agreement on the meaning of hate speech than on the definition of an internet troll. One person's heartfelt opinion or religious belief might be another's hate-filled rant. By the same token, nobody has the universal authority to float above the fray and make impartial decisions about which form of words to punish or prohibit. Everybody has an agenda and interests of their own. And control-freak governments and judges will always take requests to restrict one kind of speech as an invitation to restrict another.

The hard truth is that, to be free, freedom of speech and thought must include the right to hate who you choose – just as much as to love who you want. To defend free speech but not the freedom to spout 'hate speech' is a contradiction in terms. Don't you just hate it when your no-brainer turns out to be nonsense?

'Check your privilege before you speak to me.'
Perhaps those who use this excuse could check their self-righteousness before they say that. Free speech is a right for all, not a privilege to be restricted to a few – whether they be the lords of the manor or the activists of the transgender lobby.

This is one of the newer generation of coded assaults on free speech. It expresses the notion that only certain people should have the right to speak about certain issues, that the 'privileged' should not presume to talk about issues of oppression or inequality. It is about identity groups claiming a monopoly on the truth about themselves. So don't talk about racism unless you're black, but black men have no business sticking their noses into black women's affairs. Woe betide any man or 'person without a uterus' who wants to express an opinion on abortion, or a 'cisgender' individual of either sex who dares to disagree with the transgender lobby's self-definition.

The demand to 'check your privilege' is posed as an anti-elitist attempt to give a voice to the voiceless. The irony is it expresses an inverse elitism, a wish among some to keep free speech for themselves. Once upon a time we were told that public discussion of important matters was the exclusive preserve of kings and cardinals, barons and bishops. Now we have a new version of that selective attitude to speech, updated for the age of identity politics. The effect is the same – to turn speech itself into a privilege, not a right, to be granted only to the 'right' class of people.

The demand to restrict speech on these issues stands in stark contrast to the attitude of past campaigners for black, women's or lesbian and gay rights, who understood that winning free speech for all was the necessary precondition for their liberation. The language may have changed, but the truth remains that making speech less free is no path to liberation for anybody.

'Rights come with responsibilities.'

No, they do not. Otherwise they cease to be liberties belonging to us by right, and transmogrify into concessions granted by governments and judges with conditions attached like chains.

It would be good to hope that everybody might use their right to free speech in a responsible fashion, and take responsibility for what they say or write. That does not mean, however, that they should be restricted to saying only what others approve of. The right to free speech has to mean that other people are not responsible to you or me for what they say or think. Nobody has to pass an ethics test or gain a licence in logical argument in order to qualify for freedom of expression. If we have a responsibility it is only to speak what we believe to be the truth – and leave others free to disagree.

'We have the right to feel safe and comfortable.'

If you're talking about the need to feel safe from violence and comfortable in decent housing, fine. But as a demand to be protected against other people's opinions – that 'right' is wrong.

The fashion for 'safe spaces' in universities is code for turning campuses into gated comfort zones, where nobody has to confront challenging ideas or opinions. That's the opposite of the open-minded debate and inquiry upon which university life depends. Safe-space policies and the demand to be 'comfortable' are used to demand the exclusion of any speech students claim to find upsetting, whether that be alleged Islamist extremism or alleged Islamophobia.

These measures risk turning campuses into soporific cocoons, where students and academics are protected from anything that might wake them up or ask them to think differently. They don't just infringe on the free-speech rights of a few, but rob the rest of the freedom to listen and judge for themselves – and possibly even to change their minds. To use 'feeling comfortable' as an excuse for restricting free speech puts the risk of a tummy upset above the principle of moral autonomy. It treats students – young adults – as a cross between helpless toddlers and stuck-in-their-ways pensioners. Free speech and open debate can certainly be uncomfortable, and you are entitled to shelter from it if you prefer. But that does not give you the right to stick your fingers in everybody else's ears so they can't listen either.

'We cannot tolerate intolerance.'

This is really a cute way of justifying censorship in the name of freedom from oppression. That ought to be an intolerable twisting of the truth.

An avowed refusal to tolerate intolerance has been used to ban speakers or adverts accused of anything from homophobia to Islamophobia. It brings to mind Big Brother's official language, Newspeak, from Orwell's *Nineteen Eighty-Four*, which is notorious for making words such as 'freedom' mean their opposite.

True tolerance means allowing the expression of ideas and opinions which you find objectionable, including those that are intolerant of other people's freedoms. It does not mean stamping on 'intolerant' views with a politically correct boot. But neither does it mean pussy-footing around the problem and allowing everybody to express their prejudices with impunity. True tolerance is about bringing it all out into the open, to allow the fullest and freest debate. It is about enabling a battle of opinions to the bitter end. By contrast, the fashion for intolerance in the name of tolerance means closing down that debate before it has even begun. The only tolerable response to bad speech is more speech, not just those two little words 'zero tolerance'.

'That's x-phobic!'

It seems madness to try to brand opinions you disagree with as mental health problems.

There is an apparent epidemic of phobias in Anglo-American society, and it is spreading. First the emphasis was on the problem of homophobia, then on the rise of Islamophobia, now there is talk of transphobia, Afrophobia, fatphobia, whatevaphobia. A phobia, lest we forget, is defined as 'an irrational fear of or aversion to something'. To call the expression of different ideas 'phobic' means to damn them not just as objectionable opinions, but as symptoms of a psychiatric disorder. It says that your own views on, say, Islam or homosexuality are so normal and unquestionable that any opposite opinion must be the product of a disturbed mind. And of course there is no point debating with the opinions of the 'phobics', since they are irrational and dangerous. Far better to muzzle and quarantine the carriers, as one would mad dogs suspected of hydrophobia.

If there is a 'phobia' on display here (though we should perhaps hesitate to use the word), it is surely the fear and loathing of other people's speech and non-conformist opinions. It might even look like a symptom of your own narcissistic personality disorder to imagine that anybody with the opposite strongly held views to you must be slightly mad. It is worth recalling that the authoritarian Stalinist regime in the old Soviet Union was keen on accusing its political critics of mental health problems and imprisoning them in psychiatric institutions. That seems a poor role model for anybody interested in challenging prejudice today.

'You're a Denier!'

To accuse your opponents of telling lies about an issue is no excuse for denying them their right to freedom of speech.

Along with all those multiplying phobias, there appears to be a dangerous epidemic of denial across Western societies. First the focus was on the problem of Holocaust denial. Now we are also warned that public debate has been infected by climate-change denial, racism denial, rape denial, inequality denial and many more variants up to and including 'denial denial'.

And as with allegations of 'phobia', the consequences of accusing somebody of denial are far-reaching. It means that they have crossed the line from expressing an honest opinion to acting out a psychiatric disorder. 'Denial' is now bandied about in the language of psychiatry, to mean that somebody is suppressing some unquestionable truth about the Holocaust or climate change – denying facts which everybody knows are true. As such, there is deemed to be no point in debating with them. Instead their views – and possibly their persons – should be locked away to prevent them doing any harm.

Yet even if you think they are twisted liars, those branded deniers should still have the right to free speech for reasons of both principle and practice. In principle, free speech must be defended for all or it will be safe for none at all; and it is the extreme or unpalatable opinion that needs protecting most. Defend free speech for them and the mainstream will look after itself. In practice, the only way to be sure of the truth is to allow it to be tested from all directions. Of course we know that the Holocaust is an historical fact. But that does not mean its history is beyond debate. Far from affirming the truth, to try to silence critics and opponents instead by beating them with the allegation of 'denial' inevitably raises the question: what have you got to hide?

'Your words oppress me – that's microaggression.'

The notion that words can oppress makes a nonsense of the concept in the present and insults the struggles of the past. Oppression involves the denial of equal legal and social rights to a group. That is what women, black people, gays and colonial peoples fought against in the past, often suffering and even dying in the struggle for liberty. It does not mean somebody being a bit rude or making you feel uncomfortable with the way they talk.

When racist language was commonplace in UK and US society, it was a reflection of the real power and respectability of racism in our politics and culture. Now that racism is no longer respectable, and old-fashioned racist language is rarely heard, we are left with a ghost struggle against often-ordinary words which are accused of 'unwitting racism'. The concept of 'microaggression' takes things a step further, finding oppression in the most minor interactions of everyday life – such as somebody using the pronoun 'him'.

Words can be weapons in a battle of ideas or a slanging match. But words are not literally weapons with which to do violent harm, or magic spells with the power to oppress. We need to give more power to speech, not less, and set it free to debate issues from the real meaning of oppression to the correct use of language.

'By calling for a ban on your speech, we're exercising our free speech!'

Are we living in such a looking-glass world that the reverse-Voltaires can seriously claim their loud demands for censorship demonstrate free speech in action?

It is a hallmark of what I have called the silent war on free speech that few want to admit that they are against that liberty in principle. The reverse-Voltaires insist that their attempts to restrict what somebody else can say are not really an attack on his freedom of speech. This reaches its nadir in the argument that the ones demanding a speaker be 'No Platformed' into silence are true champions of free speech. They are exercising the inalienable right to express their opinion, which just happens to be that you should not be allowed to express yours.

Anybody does indeed have the right to use their freedom of speech in order to argue against it. Free speech is for fanatics and hysterics, too. And anybody has the right to deliver a forceful response to what somebody else has to say. Although it is normally considered good practice to hear what that might be first.

But nobody has the 'right' to deny freedom of expression to somebody else in the name of freedom, however objectionable their opinion might appear. To try to do so is an act both of censoriousness and of stupidity, since it denies us the chance to decide for ourselves and does nothing to refute the other's argument. Nor will the argument wash that 'it's not censorship because it's not the state doing it'. The informal, unofficial censorship exercised by the online mob of reverse-Voltaires is the most commonplace and pernicious threat in the age of the silent war on free speech.

However you try to dress it up, demanding No Platform for opinions you dislike is the reactionary action of cowards (who don't trust their own ability to win an argument) and prigs (who don't think others should be allowed to hear naughty words). You are free to call it the exercise of free speech if you choose. Just as long as we're free to tell you what you can do with your No Platform placards.

'Free speech is all well and good but you don't have the right to insult other people's beliefs.'
In fact if you don't have the right to be offensive to others' beliefs – and if others don't have the right to do the same to you – then free speech is not 'all well and good'. It would be worthless and dead.

The right to be offensive is not, as the Pope seems to think, about being able to curse somebody's mother with impunity. It does not mean making a virtue of personal insults.

It is primarily about the right to offend other people's beliefs, by challenging their fundamental worldview and questioning what they deem the unquestionable. And it is not only, as some seemed to think after *Charlie Hebdo*, about the right to offend Islam. No belief-system should be immune from being interrogated and offended, be it fascism or radical feminism, flat-earthism or environmentalism.

The right to be offensive is not an optional bolt-on to free speech, to be 'butted' out of existence leaving the principle intact. What is 'free' about speech if we are only permitted to say that which others find agreeable? Without fighting for the heretical right to offend against society's consensus views and to question the unquestionable orthodoxies of the age, many of the great political, cultural, scientific or artistic breakthroughs that we now take for granted would have been hard to imagine.

There is nothing big or clever about being offensive as an end in itself; but as a means to striving for the truth, whether through politics or comedy, it is often unavoidable and always indispensable.

'Trigger Warning'

Trigger Warnings themselves speak volumes about what is wrong with contemporary attitudes to freedom of speech. They encapsulate the attitude that potentially hurt feelings are more important than universal free speech, and that freedom of expression is not a right but a privilege that should come with conditions, chains and warnings not to step off the edge of the known world.

Let the spreading appearance of those letters 'TW' be a warning to those who appreciate free speech as the most important liberty of all. Trigger Warnings that hold a pistol to the head of free speech should have us all reaching for our metaphorical guns to fight for the right to think what we like, and say what we think.

Notes

Introduction to the concise edition
1. www.frontpagemag.com/2015/truthrevolt-org/andrew-klavan-attack-of-the-but-heads/.
2. 'Isis influence on web promts second thoughts on First Amendment', *New York Times*, 28 December 2015.

1: A few things we forgot about free speech
1. Thomas Paine, *The Age of Reason*, 1794, from *Selected Writings*, The Franklin Library, 1979, p. 236.
2. Orwell, 'The Freedom of the Press', 1945, cited in Appendix I to George Orwell, *Animal Farm*, Secker & Warburg, 1987.
3. Quoted mediaite.com, 15 January 2015.
4. *Gettysburg Times*, 24 June 1999.
5. Benedict de Spinoza, *A Theological-Political Treatise*, 1670, http://www.sacred-texts.com/phi/spinoza/treat/tpt28.htm
6. 'A Plea for Free Speech in Boston', 1860, classiclit.about.com/library/bl-etexts/fdouglass/bl-fdoug-freespeech.htm
7. David Feldman, *Civil Liberties and Human Rights in England and Wales*, Oxford University Press, 2002, p. 753.
8. ibid., p. 752.
9. ibid., p. 770.
10. Cited in Anthony Lewis, *Freedom for the Thought That We Hate: a Biography of the First Amendment*, Basic Books, New York, 2009, p. 107.
11. J. S. Mill, *On Liberty*, 1859, Oxford World's Classics, 1998, p. 9.

2: The age of the reverse-Voltaires
1. www.frontpagemag.com/2015/truthrevolt-org/andrew-klavan-attack-of-the-but-heads/

2. Mark Johnson and Conor Gearty, 'Civil liberties and the challenge of terrorism', in Park, A., J. Curtice, K. Thomson, M. Phillips and M. Johnson (eds), *British Social Attitudes: the 23rd Report*, Sage, London, 2007, p. 168.

3. http://www.newseum.org/wp-content/uploads/2014/08/connect_blog_SOFA14-infographic.jpg

4. Evelyn Beatrice Hall, *The Friends of Voltaire*, 1907 (originally published in 1906 under the pseudonym S. G. Tallentyre).

5. Philip Johnston, *Feel Free to Say It*, Civitas, 2013, p. 7.

6. Nadine Strossen, *Defending Pornography: Free Speech, Sex and the Fight for Women's Rights*, NYU Press Paperback, 2000 edition, pp. 41–2.

7. Karl Marx, 'Censorship', *Rheinische Zeitung*, no. 135, 15 May 1842.

8. For a full list of the signatories see Hacked Off website, 18 March 2014, http://hackinginquiry.org/mediareleases/declarationmarch18/

9. Cited in Catherine Bowen, *The Lion and the Throne*, Hamish Hamilton, 1957, p. 298.

10. Thomas Hobbes, *Leviathan*, Part One 1651, Wildside Press 2008 edition, p. 61.

11. Twitchy.com, 30 April 2014.

12. 'Policing private speech: the new inquisition', Spiked-online.com, 22 May 2014, http://www.spiked-online.com/freespeechnow/fsn_article/policing-private-speech-the-new-inquisition#.VRa86uFsycE

13. George Orwell, *Nineteen Eighty-Four* (1949), Penguin 1979 edition, p. 169.

3: A short history of free-speech heretics

1. Lord Denning, former Master of the Rolls, cited magnacarta800th.com/schools/downloads-and-resources/magna-carta-quotations/

2. family.twinn.co.uk/The-Trial-of-John-Twyn-for-High-Treason-16634.html

3. Cited in Tzvetan Todorov, *In Defence of the Enlightenment*, Atlantic Books, 2010, p. 70.

4. David A. Copeland, *The Idea of a Free Press: the Enlightenment and Its Unruly Legacy*, Northwestern University Press, 2006, p. 39.

5. Arlene W. Saxonhouse, *Free Speech and Democracy in Ancient Athens*, Cambridge University Press, New York, 2006, p. 105.

6. ibid., p. 212.

7. http://files.libertyfund.org/pll/quotes/51.html

8. Cited in George Rudé, *Wilkes and Liberty*, Lawrence and Wishart 1983 edition, p. 162.

9. Louis Kronenberger, *The Extraordinary Mr Wilkes*, New English Library, 1974, p. 33.

10. ibid., p. 186.

11. Leonard Levy, cited in Walter Berns, *The First Amendment and the Future of American Democracy*, Gateway Editions, Illinois, 1985, pp. 84–5.
12. ibid., p. 117.
13. Karl Marx, 'On Freedom of the Press', first published 1842 in the *Rheinische Zeitung*, www.marxists.org/archive/marx/works/1842/free-press/
14. J. S. Mill, *On Liberty*, 1859, Oxford World's Classics, 1998, p. 21.
15. Michael Kent Curtis, *Free Speech, 'The People's Darling Privilege': Struggles for Freedom of Expression in American History*, Duke University Press, 2000, p. 117.
16. *New York Times Co v. Sullivan*, https://supreme.justia.com/cases/federal/us/376/254/case.html
17. *Brandenburg v. Ohio*, https://supreme.justia.com/cases/federal/us/395/444/case.html

4: '… but words will *always* hurt me'

1. Stephen Fry, *Moab is My Washpot: an Autobiography*, Hutchinson, 1997, p. 113.
2. Richard King, *On Offence: the Politics of Indignation*, Scribe Publications, 2013, p. 42.
3. Thomas Carlyle, 'Sir Walter Scott', in *Carlyle's Works*, vols 15–16, New York International Book Company, 1869, p. 407.
4. J. S. Mill, *On Liberty*, 1859, Oxford World's Classics, 1998, p. 14.
5. Frank Furedi, *On Tolerance: a Defence of Moral Independence*, Continuum Books, 2011, p. 153.
6. Ibid.
7. Thomas Jefferson, *Notes on the State of Virginia*, 1782.
8. Cited in *National Review*, 9 January 2015.
9. http://www.glaad.org/reference/transgender
10. Frederick Douglass, 'A Plea for Free Speech in Boston', 1860, classiclit.about.com/library/bl-etexts/fdouglass/bl-fdoug-freespeech.htm
11. Cited King, *On Offence*, p. 221.

5: 'There is no right to shout "Fire!" in a crowded theatre'

1. https://supreme.justia.com/cases/federal/us/249/47/; Walter Berns, *The First Amendment and the Future of American Democracy*, Gateway Editions, Illinois, 1985, pp. 150–5; Anthony Lewis, *Freedom for the Thought That We Hate*, Basic Books, New York, 2009, pp. 26–7.
2. https://supreme.justia.com/cases/federal/us/279/644/case.html; Lewis, pp. 37–8.
3. *Gitlow v. New York*, 1925.

6: 'Mind your Ps, Qs, Ns and Ys'

1. *Daily Mail*, 30 April 2013.
2. *LA Times*, 29 January 1999, http://articles.latimes.com/1999/jan/29/news/mn-2884
3. https://twitter.com/harrietharman/status/462271405024108544
4. www.goodreads.com/quotes/tag/freedom-of-speech?page=3

7: 'Free speech is just a licence for the mass media to brainwash the public'

1. Quoted by Guido Fawkes, 25 September 2012.
2. Karl Marx, 'On Freedom of the Press', *Rheinische Zeitung*, no. 139, 19 May 1842.
3. Professor John Carey, *The Intellectuals and the Masses: Pride and Prejudice among the Literary Intelligentsia 1880–1939*, Faber and Faber, 1992, p. 7.
4. ibid., p. 15.
5. ibid., pp. 7, 15, 121.
6. See Mick Hume, *There is No Such Thing as a Free Press*, op. cit., p. 78.
7. See Daniel J. Boorstin, *The Image: A Guide to Pseudo-events in America*, 1962 edition.
8. Copeland, *The Idea of a Free Press*, op. cit., p. 99.
9. Orwell, 'The Freedom of the Press', 1945, cited in Appendix I to George Orwell, *Animal Farm*, Secker & Warburg, 1987, p. 100.
10. Karl Marx, 'On Freedom of the Press', *Rheinische Zeitung*, no. 135, 15 May 1842.

8: 'Liars and Holocaust deniers do not deserve to be heard'

1. Stephen Snobelen, 'Isaac Newton, heretic: the strategies of a Nicodemite', *British Journal for the History of Science*, 1999, vol. 32, p. 381.
2. Arthur Versluis, *The New Inquisitions; Heretic-Hunting and the Intellectual Origins of Modern Totalitarianism*, Oxford University Press, 2006, p. 7.
3. Deborah Lipstadt, 'Denial should be defeated by facts, not laws', *Spiked*, 16 July 2007.
4. ibid., p. 24.
5. *Research Fortnight*, 16 February 2011, http://www.researchresearch.com/index.php?option=com_news&template=rr_2col&view=article&articleId=1032320

The fear of free speech

1. Rosa Luxemburg, *The Russian Revolution*, 1918.
2. http://www.imdb.com/title/tt0117318/quotes
3. *Whitney v. California*, 1927, www.law.cornell.edu/supremecourt/text/274/357